FOOTBALLERS AND BUSINESSMEN

Footballers
and
Businessmen:

THE ORIGINS OF
PROFESSIONAL SOCCER
IN ENGLAND

Steven Tischler

HOLMES & MEIER PUBLISHERS, INC.
NEW YORK   LONDON

First published in the United States of America 1981 by
Holmes & Meier Publishers, Inc.
30 Irving Place
New York, N.Y. 10003

Great Britain:
Holmes & Meier Publishers, Ltd.
131 Trafalgar Road
Greenwich, London SE10 9TX

Library of Congress Cataloging in Publication Data

Tischler, Steven,
    Footballers and businessmen.

    Bibliography: p. 145
    Includes index.
    1. Soccer—England—History.   2. Soccer—Social
aspects—England.   3. Soccer—Economic aspects—England
4. Professional sports—England.   I. Title.
GV944.G7T57   1980   796.334'0942   80–26656

ISBN 0–8419–0658–0

MANUFACTURED IN THE UNITED STATES OF AMERICA

For my parents

Contents

Illustrations follow page 104.

Acknowledgments

Many people, most notably Tom Angress, Gene Lebovics and other members of the Stony Brook history department, helped me to recognize the relevance of history as a discipline and to ask the types of questions posed in this book. Stephen Koss was a rigorous dissertation advisor at Columbia who helped me to clarify my thinking concerning the relationship of sports and leisure to English society. Jacob Smit assisted in the formulation of an analytical framework for the manuscript in its early stages.

Several colleagues read parts of the manuscript, and I would like to thank Danny Freeman, Harold Fruchtbaum, Mark Kesselman, Robert McCaughey, Standish Meacham, Joyce Rieglehaupt, James Walvin, Theodore Wendt, and Joseph White for their interest and suggestions. Wray Vamplew provided extremely useful insights and bibliographic references, and Bill Baker gave the completed manuscript an especially thorough and most helpful reading. Tony Mason's *Association Football and English Society 1863–1915* appeared just as this book went to press; I was therefore unable to benefit from his research. Readers of both works will note our differing conclusions on some important points and will recognize that the subject of sports in society merits further research and debate.

George Bernstein, Elissa Itzkin, and Tom Osborne passed along citations on football which they uncovered in their own research. The staffs of the British Library at the British Museum and at the Colindale Newspaper Library provided great assistance, as did the officers of the Football League and the Football Association who made available to me their libraries and minute books. Cliff Lloyd of the Professional Footballers' Association in Manchester provided warmth and hospitality along with records of his organization.

Very special thanks must go to my sister, Janet, and to Fran Zujkowski for their consistent support and thoughtfulness. English friends Karen Cooper and Philip Northcott also merit thanks for some extraordinary transatlantic assistance.

Rita Troy was most encouraging and helpful throughout the writing of this book; her advice has been invaluable. Bob Wechsler was supportive, as true friends are, during a year in London and throughout graduate school at Columbia. He provided thoughtful criticism and suggested bibliographic references.

Five years ago, my wife, Barbara, on first hearing of this project, wondered if she might help. Since that time, she more than anyone else has provided me with insights, questions and perspective which sharpened the work as a whole. And while she has been instrumental in qualitatively improving this manuscript through each of its stages, her love and support have surpassed her intellectual contribution to this work.

Introduction

The bourgeoisie has stripped of its halo every occupation hitherto honored and looked up to with reverent awe. It has converted the physician, the lawyer, the priest, the poet, the man of science, into its paid wage laborers. —Marx and Engels, *The Communist Manifesto,* 1847–1848[1]

Had Marx and Engels analyzed sports in England at the end of the nineteenth century, they might have included "athletes" among those whose activities were being increasingly governed by the demands of a market economy. Just as a nineteenth century physician, poet, or scientist relied on his art or trade for a livelihood, athletes earned their living as jockeys, cyclists, or footballers in the realm of newly professionalized sports. The evolution of the athlete coincided with the transformation of English sports from casual amateur pastimes to serious competitions wherein sports entrepreneurs and professional athletes coexisted, albeit often on uneasy terms.

Industrialization, which had brought about a decline in numerous plebeian recreations by the early decades of the nineteenth century, also helped to extend cash nexus relationships to popular recreations. At the end of the nineteenth century, the operation of many leisure activities incorporated and buttressed prevailing commercial practices of the larger society.[2] Participants in the new entertainments increasingly wore the uniform or costume of the professional athlete, dancer, or singer.

The business structure which emerged in sports resembled that of other enterprises in late Victorian England. The better football teams, for instance, were financed by shareholders. The product offered for sale to the public was sporting entertainment which embodied matches among working-class men who specialized in scoring goals against an opponent. That football playing was a highly skilled profession by the 1880s only underlines the degree to which this pastime had become a business. Competition among teams for gate revenues and profits was yet another commercial aspect of the new version of football, especially among teams which belonged to the Football League. As in the world of factories and shops, those football clubs which were well financed and efficiently managed survived.

During the eighteenth and nineteenth centuries, dramatic changes occurred in both the styles of play and in the social profile and status of football players. Three distinct varieties of the game existed within this time frame: first, a plebeian version flourished before the coming of the Industrial Revolution; next, a well-organized and codified form evolved at England's public schools in the first half of the nineteenth century; and commercial-professional football was created in the last decades of the century. A principal aim of this inquiry is to explain why one form and not another predominated in a particular period.

The radical contrast in styles of play and in backgrounds of participants before and after industrialization prompts a reconsideration of previous analyses of football and of sports in general. Until the 1930s, scholars paid scant attention to the functions of sports or to their changing roles over time.[3] Although vivid accounts of football play have provided historians with a picture of contests and players,[4] purely descriptive histories have left unanswered the questions of why some played football and others did not, and why the game assumed various forms over the centuries.

The publication of Johan Huizinga's seminal *Homo Ludens: A Study of the Play Element in Culture* (1939) created a new point of departure for the study of sports. With his assertion that a "play urge" is elemental to the human psyche, Huizinga employed a study of motivation as an analytical tool. Other scholars subsequently have amplified his theories in a number of important works.[5]

However provocative their ideas, and whatever their contribution to an understanding of the internal dimensions of play and games, the sociologists and philosophers who have incorporated Huizinga's approach have not been concerned with the changing nature and function of sports in society. The metamorphosis of play patterns cannot be elucidated solely by reference to the psychic needs of athletes outside a clearly defined historical context. Such factors as the emotional rewards of engaging in a pastime may help to explain recreational preferences during a given period, but they cannot clarify why disjunctures occur in the frequency and style of play over time. The play urge helps to account for the joys of athletic participation in any century, but it fails to provide insights into why, in sports such as football, some classes comprise the body of participants while others are excluded. Nor can the play urge by itself shed light on the issue of why the social origins of players change when a new version of a game supersedes an older one. It cannot reveal a dynamic for the evolution of a sport.

A study of fundamental shifts in social and economic relationships which permeated the domain of recreation is a useful starting point for an attempt to transcend the limitations of the Huizinga school. The history of football in England provides a test case for a theory of sports development which emphasizes these changing arrangements. The version of football which peasants, artisans, and cottage workers played in preindustrial England corresponded to the natural rhythm of work and play activities in which relatively few restrictions or regulations existed. As the process of industrialization overwhelmed plebeian society, football as it had been played was no longer feasible. Peasant-artisan football declined drastically as a result of circumstances unrelated to the recreational preferences of its former participants.

Another form of football evolved in an environment which stood in sharp contrast to the peasant-artisan community. The game experienced a renaissance in England's public schools during the first half of the nineteenth century, when the need for an efficient, well-trained bureaucracy prompted the creation of a codified, organized version of football. Educators took pains to distinguish schoolboy football from the cruder plebeian version so that public school football would be appropriate in form and style to the upper echelons of society and would be a suitable vehicle for the education of young gentlemen.

In the 1880s, businessmen club directors introduced a new version of the game which reflected their aims and interests. The metamorphosis of business relations in football affected the social profile of team rosters, helped initiate the creation of League football, and generated trade union militancy among professional players. The growth of football along commercial-professional lines was not a spontaneous occurrence. It was the result of calculated nurturing by entrepreneurs who extended to football an ethos which touched numerous endeavors outside of sports.

The changes in football aroused considerable comment and nostalgia. Contrasts in style and participants were described with passion as one version of the game was threatened by the rise of a new one. Such concern was particularly apparent in the diatribes of old-boy players in the 1880s whose brand of football was being undermined by the spread of the commercial-professional game. Less embittered observers were also struck by the radical changes in the sport over a generation. In the middle of the nineteenth century, football had been played at a slower pace, and even national tournaments seemed "quiet and unobtrusive." Football clubs in those days had had "time to grow." By 1905, however,

> the wealthy brewer and prosperous builder combine to form a company, lay out capital in the provision of a ground that is up-to-date, purchase or otherwise collect together an array of "talent," and take the football world by storm. Where once clubs grew slowly and quietly, they now spring up like "mushrooms in a night."[6]

The development of a commercialized, professional version of football elicited articles in the late nineteenth-century sporting press which seemed designed to amuse readers by reminding them that their well-organized, regulated game had been a raucous fray some centuries earlier.[7] While journalistic reporting of this type was of a believe-it-or-not nature, some writers made special note of the fraternal feelings among professional players, which evoked preindustrial play patterns. The anachronistic quality of such collegiality to the commercial-professional version of football was often in evidence at Christmas reunions among professionals. One journalist described the "clannish spirit" of such gatherings of Scottish players employed by the professional teams of the Lancashire mill towns. In spite of the atmosphere of a "family gathering" as fellow Scotsmen smoked and drank together, it was clear that the warmth of the occasion was fleeting. Once players returned to the football pitch and donned their team uniforms, they were advised that,

> as W.S. Gilbert says in one of his plays, "Twa pund is twa pund," and even the grasp of friendship has to moult a feather when claims of business stand in the way.[8]

This book will examine more closely the nature of such "claims of business" and analyze how they arose. "Claims of business" were absent from plebeian and schoolboy football, but represented a new and important development in sports by the end of the nineteenth century.

Numerous other contrasts appear among commercial-professional football and its predecessors. Football at its most advanced level of performance after the early 1880s was controlled not by the actual players, as in the plebeian and schoolboy games, but by nonplaying "officials" or entrepreneurs. Further, a separation emerged between participants and spectators which was strengthened by the evolution of football as a paying business venture.

Plebeian and schoolboy football each had accentuated and furthered the separation of classes at play. Plebeian football was restricted to the "lower orders," while upper-class males comprised the bulk of the practitioners of the schoolboy game. The commercial-professional version possessed some unique features in this regard, for this brand of football invited the participation of men from both working-class and bourgeois backgrounds. For the first time, people from different classes were directly and simultaneously involved on a significant scale in the development of football, although their different roles served to underline class distinctions. The larger societal antagonisms which had been reflected in the fact that football was exclusive to plebeian and later patrician participants, now were manifested in employer-employee tensions. Middle-class club directors and working-class players stood in essentially the same relationship to one another as did members of these classes outside of sports. The evolution of labor relations in football became as fundamental to the history of the game as the competition for League and Cup championships.

The association of sports and business may seem contradictory, even after a century of widespread commercialized sports events. That there has been a change in our perceptions and expectations of sports, particularly at the more advanced levels of competition, is hardly a revelation. What remains to be done is to explain why this change in popular perceptions and expectations has occurred. By focusing on the evolution of football in England and the social and economic forces shaping its contours, the impact and dynamic of change in sports will be more clearly understood.

Notes

1. Karl Marx and Frederick Engels, in *Selected Works* (New York: International Publishers, 1968), p. 38.

2. Gareth Stedman Jones has alluded to an "entrepreneurial business" which became "more and more organized and monopolistic" in his discussion of late nineteenth-century music halls. See "Working-Class Culture and Working-Class Politics in London, 1870–1900," *Journal of Social History* (Summer, 1974), p. 495.

3. Thorstein Veblen's treatment of sports in *The Theory of the Leisure Class* is an exception.

4. Joseph Strutt in *The Sports and Pastimes of the People of England* (London, 1801; reprint, Bath: Firecrest Publishers, 1969) and Robert MacGregor in *Pastimes and Players* (London: Chatto and Windus, 1881) include comprehensive descriptions of a variety of English sports. Francis P. Magoun in "The History of Football from the Beginnings to 1871" (*Kolner-Anglistische Arbeiten.* Bochum-Langendreer, 1938) brought to light numerous examples of football play which have been appropriated in subsequent histories of the game.

5. See, for instance, articles by John Loy and Gerald Kenyon in their anthology, *Sport, Culture and Society* (New York: Macmillan, 1969); Paul Weiss' *Sport: A Philosophic Inquiry* (Carbondale: Southern Illinois University Press, 1969); and Roger Caillois' *Man, Play and Games* (New York: Free Press, 1961).

6. Alfred Gibson and William Pickford, *Association Football and the Men Who Made It* (London: Caxton, 1905), pp. 45–46.

7. See, for instance, an article about "old fashioned football" in the 16 March 1886 issue of the *Athletic News* (p. 8), a sports journal published weekly in Manchester.

8. *Athletic News*, 31 December 1884, p. 4.

CHAPTER ONE

Plebeian and Schoolboy Football

Football's popularity among different social groups over time owes much to basic sporting principles. The competitive objective of moving a ball from point to point against opposing defenses remained constant in plebeian, schoolboy, and commercial-professional football. A "kick" was a "kick" among football players of all types, just as a quarter note was a quarter note in a sixteenth-century folk song and in a nineteenth-century symphony.

While fundamental similarities exist between upper- and lower-class cultural expression, the particular form that such expression assumes is socially conditioned. The preindustrial peasants' appreciation of the jig contrasted sharply to their estrangement from the *Gigue* composed for royal courts, despite the common musical content of both forms. The existence of ineffable qualities which gave rise to shared musical characteristics is problematic. What can be discerned, however, is that musical forms and techniques were appropriated and developed differently by different classes. A comparison of the jig danced at village celebrations and a *Gigue* composed by George Frederick Handel for a chamber ensemble reveals the divergence.

In the same way, schoolboy football diverged from the plebeian variety, despite their common play objective. Each game provided psychic benefits, as reflected in contemporary accounts of player enthusiasm. But while the human "play urge" may help to account for the lasting popularity of certain sports, the motivational factor alone explains very little. The challenge for social historians of sports is to explain how and why the same activity can follow divergent lines among various groups in different periods. English football was alternately the possession of the plebeian and patrician classes; it was an anarchic contest and a finely codified encounter; it served as an aspect of popular celebration and as a vehicle for discipline.

The decline of both the plebeian and schoolboy versions of football played a critical role in the emergence of the commercial-professional game. By the time commercial-professional football was introduced and refined, the growth of a market economy had already circumscribed traditional recreations. With the decline of many leisure activities that had thrived in an earlier period, commercialized sports and games could be introduced virtually without competition from recreational activities which were no longer feasible in an industrializing society. The story of the growth and decline of earlier forms of football forms a backdrop against which an analysis of commercial-professional football and the cash nexus relationships in leisure pursuits at the end of the nineteenth century can be presented.

The present-day observer might find it unusual that the boisterous clashes fought between the late medieval period and the early nineteenth century were called "football." This game entailed little use of the foot, and tightly wrapped rags or animal bladders sufficed for a ball. There was little dribbling or passing, and sheer brawn and pure speed afoot were more highly valued attributes than the agility, teamwork, and coordination required of modern soccer players. Yet, until relatively recently, this anarchic fray among peasants, artisans, and cottage workers *was* football,[1] one sport among many in a society deeply marked by custom and less regulated by precise time demands than modern society.[2]

Two important variables which influenced the use of leisure time were the pace of preindustrial life and the virtual exclusiveness in the recreational experience of different classes. The extent to which peasants and artisans maintained a degree of autonomy over their work largely determined when, where, and how they established their pastimes. Edward Thompson observed that deeply entrenched preindustrial work patterns provided a strong basis for a "vigorous and licensed popular culture."[3]

The notion of class exclusiveness helps explain differences in style between patrician recreations and those of the preindustrial working classes. Occasionally, common folk rubbed shoulders with members of the aristocracy and gentry at horse races and boxing matches, although J. H. Plumb has minimized these points of contact by citing measures which were taken to keep recreations exclusive.[4] Peter Burke, who argued that earlier there had been a degree of aristocratic participation in some popular pastimes, noted a "withdrawal" on the part of England's upper classes between 1500 and 1800, and their growing preference for more refined drama, dance, and sport.[5] Plebeian attendance at feast day attractions such as races and fights was distinct from upper-class interest in a match, as the latter often was tied to a substantial wager on the outcome. In the rare instances where upper- and lower-class players participated in the same sport during the early modern period, they were separated through the assignment of positions. In cricket, for instance, peasants and domestic servants bowled for their higher-bred counterparts. Generally, different styles of play were nurtured and supported by the upper and lower classes.

Descriptions of preindustrial sports in Joseph Strutt's *The Sports and Pastimes of the People of England* (1801) help to confirm the notion of class exclusiveness. Strutt observed that the game of shovelboard, "though now considered as exceedingly vulgar, and practised by lower classes of people, was formerly in great repute among the nobility and gentry."[6] Tennis was forbidden "to the common folk during the reigns of Henry VII and Henry VIII," who themselves played this game. At the beginning of the seventeenth century, the hurling of weighted objects seemed to have "lost [its] relish among the higher classes of people," and Strutt cited a contemporary who wrote that "throwing the hammer" was "not so well beseeming nobility."[7]

In describing the decline of preindustrial football, Strutt noted that it had been "formerly much in vogue among the common people of England."[8] Numerous references confirm that football was played by the "common people," while descriptions of active participation in the game by members of the upper class are conspicuously absent.

Class prejudices regarding football prompted John Strype to comment in 1720 that "the ball is used by Noblemen and Gentlemen in Tennis Courts, and by People of meaner sort in the open Fields and Streets."[9] His observation has been endorsed by Francis Magoun, whose "History of Football from the Beginnings to 1871" has provided a starting point for much recent research on the game. Magoun concluded that preindustrial football was "through and through a game of the people and is more than frowned upon as a pastime for gentlefolk."[10] Alexander Barclay described "sturdie plowmen" playing football in a sixteenth century poem,[11] and Edmund Waller's poetry in the next century alluded to shepherds who enjoyed the game.[12] There are numerous references to yeoman, husbandman, and rural artisan footballers, often in the context of judicial condemnation after rough and destructive matches.[13] Provincial colliers were described as avid football players,[14] as were urban workers in several trades.[15]

Instances of football play were recorded by literate observers who happened upon a match, and these probably represent only a small portion of the games actually played. Preindustrial work regimens permitted numerous opportunities for football. The harvest, a primary determinant of obligations during this era, created periods of intensive labor interspersed with feast days which marked the season. Football was often played as part of such celebrations, and it was also popular after the crop had been harvested, when there was generally more time for leisure.

Weddings and coronations, events which did not have a regular place on the holiday calendar, included a variety of sports and games, among them football. In addition, Malcolmson has described how the traditional holiday calendar encouraged a plethora of pastimes.[16] One day alone, Shrove Tuesday, provided Magoun with material for an entire chapter in which he depicted football matches among peasants and artisans as part of the celebration prior to Lent.[17]

An even more predictable occasion for football was the Sabbath. Observers often alluded to Sunday football to decry the violation of God's law. Occasionally, the players did not wait for the termination of services to begin play, which prompted exchanges such as the following in the *Lacedemonian Mercury* in 1692:

> *Query 6.* Whether it is not a sure sign that David Jones is a good preacher, since the people follow him so?
> *Answ.* Not at all! For in the late Frost we have seen a Football in the streets attended with a more numerous mob.[18]

The popularity of the game at the expense of Sabbath observance contributed to puritan hostility to football and other recreations, as expressed in this refrain from the seventeenth century which warned,

Who ever on Sonday Will Practis playing at Ball,
It may be before Monday the Devil will Have you all.[19]

Considerable doubt exists among historians concerning the effectiveness of puritan preaching against sports after the Interregnum. After this period of enforced moral discipline, customary pastimes were embraced once again; the maypole and the royal standard, commented Brailsford, were raised together.[20] Despite puritan doctrine, recreations were, according to Malcolmson, "thriving, deeply rooted, and widely practiced."[21] Malcolmson devoted considerable attention to the survival of feasts, fairs, and other holidays which were occasions for football play through the eighteenth century.

Popular recreations were also adapted to the system of domestic manufacture. The weekly delivery of unfinished products and collection of completed articles created a relatively autonomous work and leisure week. The spirit of Saint Monday, or the extended weekend, generally reigned in districts where domestic manufacture existed until the coming of the Industrial Revolution. Thus, a cottage worker could produce unsupervised at whatever pace permitted the completion of the week's tasks. The irregular working day, as Thompson has noted, provided the flexibility that allowed recreation during the preindustrial period.[22]

Artisans likewise found recreational opportunities prior to the Industrial Revolution. There were instances of entire guilds participating in football games, and references to individual artisans playing football appear frequently. In 1546, "servants" and "apprentices" were warned in a decree to refrain from football play,[23] and in the "Diary of Jacob Bee" (1683) there is the complaint that "seven bouchers should have play'd at football with seven glovers . . . and my man Christopher went without leave to play."[24]

The literature also reflects upper-class disdain and disapproval of football and emphasizes patrician separation from the game's perennial participants. Criticism focused on the rough style of play and the existence of a large, "uncouth" following. Condemnation of the "mob's" recreational styles and the desire to set oneself apart from the "rabble" can be inferred from the early denigrations of football. The roughness associated with the game provided a gentlemanly basis for disdain, and sixteenth-century writers such as Thomas Elyot and Phillip Stubbes criticized the "mediocritie" for engaging in the "beastly fury and extreme violence" of a sport which could more aptly be considered a "bloody and murthering practice."[25] An observer of eighteenth-century Shrovetide football in Derby may well have summarized negative upper-class sentiments when he asserted that this "coarse sport" has been carried to the barbarous heights of an election contest; nay, I have known a foot-ball hero chaired through the streets like a successful member although his utmost elevation of character was no more than that of a butcher's apprentice.[26]

While local variations in "rules" existed, plebeian football was little more than a free-for-all. Indeed, pitch boundaries usually did not exist and speci-fications for the number of players per side were rare.[27] Entire villages often played over fields measured in miles, rather than yards. This was illustrated in an eighteenth-century match between rival parishes in which one goal was located one mile outside the town, while the other goal, a watermill wheel, was far-flung in the opposite direction. One side even swam with the ball in a river.[28] A match in Middlesex was not confined to the open spaces of the villages, as the ball was kicked and passed through "the most public thoroughfares, the shops and houses of which were customarily closed, and the windows barricaded with hurdles to prevent their being broken."[29] When a visitor to London in 1703 observed a particularly unruly group of people, he was reminded of how "the mob" would "break windows at football."[30] Football's reputation as an uncouth, lower-class pastime, mirrored in re-marks by contemporaries, prompted Magoun to conclude that it was rejected by the preindustrial elite, which practiced more refined diversions.

While the upper classes did not play football and often disparaged the sport, some members of the gentry and aristocracy found it opportune to lend a tacit approval to the game and its players. This may account for the survival of football through much of the early modern period. Even James I, who barred football from his court as a "rough and violent exercise," encouraged the plebeian version of the game.[31]

James' Declaration on Sports of 1618 stipulated that after church services, "our good people be not disturbed, letted, or discouraged from any lawful recreation, such as dancing . . . archery . . . leaping, vaulting, or any other harmless recreation." Only bull and bear baiting (and, "in the meaner sort of people, by law prohibited, bowling") were banned.[32] Football escaped censure in this instance, but largely because James sought to curb the power of puritan magistrates who had barred traditional Sunday amusements.

James hoped to foster a reaction against puritanism by restoring a game that was popular with a broad spectrum of the population. He appealed to the "commoner and meaner sort" who again would enjoy Sundays as they wished, "as they must apply their labour, and win their living in all working daies."[33] James' view of the game, as expressed in the ban on football and in the declaration, was consistent; a politic toleration of football did not alter his opinion of the game per se, nor of the class of men for whom he deemed it appropriate.

James' stance was emulated by some landed men of wealth who, for the next two centuries, sought to retain traditional relationships with the working population. Thus, outside Alnwick Castle, Shrovetide players had for gener-ations waited for a ball to be thrown to them over the castle walls. In 1827, when a controversy threatened the playing of the traditional match, the Duke of Northumberland provided a meadow.[34]

Persons of rank appeared at football matches as spectators and occasionally engaged in a ceremonial sanctioning of the festivities. During a Shrove Tuesday game at Derby, the players were

> encouraged by respectable persons attached to each party [who] take a surprising interest in the result of the day's sport; urging on the players with shouts, and even handing to those who are exhausted, oranges and other refreshments.[35]

On the plain of Carterhaugh in the early nineteenth century, the Duke of Buccleuch ceremoniously tossed out the ball in a contest waged by hundreds of rival clansmen.[36]

Rural notables generally were inclined to continue established customs in the countryside through the eighteenth century, and it is possible that the feasts sponsored by the gentry reenforced their prominent role in a stratified but harmonious community. The gentry's contributions to the sustenance of a plebeian culture seemed obligatory for the preservation of its reputation according to the standards of the age. G. M. Trevelyan has referred to the "substantial squires" who maintained an unchallenged "patriarchal sway" in an England as yet untouched by significant industrialization.[37] According to Trevelyan, it was a time when the wage earner both in town and country hardly resented his "want of social and political power." Instead, the "spirit of aristocracy and the spirit of popular rights seemed to have arrived at perfect harmony."[38]

Thompson and Malcolmson are among the historians who have disputed many of the conclusions drawn from this description of preindustrial class relations. They have subsumed examples of upper-class largesse into an analytical framework which emphasizes social control. There is no disputing the gentry's desire to retain its influence through displays of generosity; rather, such rituals are analyzed against a background of a more active plebeian threat to the social order. Vulnerability to social dissatisfaction necessitated conventions that could help to insure stability, and a variety of mannerisms and artifices were designed to exhibit "authority to the plebs and to extract from them deference."[39] Occasions of public patronage emanated from a society more tense than had been previously depicted; the largesse and grandeur displayed by gentlemen would alternately ingratiate and intimidate. The sanctioning ceremonies before a football match illustrated that while the upper classes sometimes lent their sponsorship, they were by no means on an equal footing with peasant and artisan players. Class differences were delineated all the more clearly through these ceremonies in which notables lent their blessings and then retreated to the sidelines.

Plebeian footballers continued to play in the face of clerical and gentlemanly deprecations, but new demands on people and work time created a social order with fewer recreational opportunities. A radical break in the continuity of leisure activities was generated by the more complete triumph of capitalist industry and agriculture during the latter part of the eighteenth century. This transformation occurred against the wishes of traditional players, but the force of change tended to overwhelm even those who actively clung to their pastimes.

Plebeian football was unsuited to an urban, commercial environment. The space that had been used for football was being converted into business sites or thoroughfares, while the violence of the game threatened property. Merchants and local officials cooperated in banning football in several areas as the pace of commerce quickened. The game was considered a disturbance of the peace in Bolton in 1790, while magistrates in Kingston-upon-Thames prosecuted players in the same decade. Officials in Hull ordered football off the streets in 1818, and the *Hull Advertiser* warned that the police had "strict orders to prevent any persons from playing at any game in the streets troublesome to the inhabitants." The Highways Act of 1835 allowed a 40 s. penalty for playing "football or any other Game 'on any Part of the said Highways."[40]

The decline of plebeian football is illustrated by events in Derby. In 1796, jurors asserted that the annual Shrovetide clash was a

> custom which has no better recommendation than its antiquity for its further continuance, is disgraceful to humanity and civilization, subversive of good order and Government and destructive of the Moral, Properties, and very Lives of our Inhabitants.[41]

A Derby resident wrote in *The Mercury* in 1844 that if fellow citizens would refrain from supporting the game and would instead "order the police to take up [players] under the Vagrant Act, we should get rid of the annual nuisance called football." In 1846, two troops of dragoons were sent to the town to prevent the playing of the Shrovetide match.[42]

The effects of industrialization on urban recreation were examined by the Select Parliamentary Committee on Walks in 1833. In its report, the committee asserted that for the previous half century, the extension of buildings and the enclosure of commons offered "little or no provision" for "Public Walks or Open Spaces, fitted to afford means of exercise or amusement to the middle or humbler classes."[43] These conclusions were based on interviews such as the one between the committee and William Fielden, M.P. for Blackburn. Fielden reiterated points raised earlier by witnesses from industrialized regions in this exchange with examiners:

> Is there any place to which the children of humbler classes may resort for any game or exercise, any of those games they have been used to on holidays?
> —None whatever.
> If they wanted a game at football there is no place, except they trespass in a field?
> —That is my notion.[44]

Deviations from a strict work schedule had been acceptable on a modest scale in preindustrial society. Edicts condemning football were not respected, as demonstrated by the continuation of peasant and artisan play well into the eighteenth century, despite the complaints of some employers. However, the Industrial Revolution generated demands of time and discipline for the working class that were qualitatively more rigorous and enforceable than those that had existed earlier. Production was closely supervised and workers no longer formulated their own schedules. As artisans and out-workers in many parts of England lost control over the pace of their work, first through competition with machines and then as extensions of them, factories superseded the cottage as the primary locus of production.

Worker control over the process of manufacture was diminished earlier in the textile regions, where mills were erected by the 1790s, than in Birmingham, where the hardware industry was not centralized until the next century. An important variable in the transformation of work and leisure was the degree of mechanization. In Birmingham, according to Douglas Reid, observation of Saint Monday persisted until the introduction of steam power on a wide scale after the 1830s, while alterations in work regimens were experienced earlier in Lancashire and Yorkshire.[45]

One characteristic of the early factory system which precluded the continuation of sports such as football was the sheer exhaustion created by the work day, sufficient to drain the energies of most people. According to M. A. Bienefeld, the "normal day" of work in a number of trades extended from 6 A.M. to 6 P.M. for six days a week through the middle decades of the nineteenth century.[46] The Factory Act of 1831 set twelve hours as the limit to the workday for cotton mill operatives who were under eighteen years of age, while workers over the age of eighteen and wage earners in other trades, such as mining, worked longer hours. It was unlikely that many workers had strength for football after a full shift, even if they retained the desire to play.

In evaluating the impact of the Industrial Revolution, historians whom Eric Hobsbawm has called "optimists" (they include John Clapham, T. S. Ashton, and R. M. Hartwell) have barely considered such themes as leisure. Nor have they weighed new behavioral norms in the work place, or the ways in which the new regimen might have affected broader attitudes and practices outside the mill or factory. While these factors are difficult to measure, and precise agreement concerning their importance is elusive, it is possible to make generalizations about the quality of life during the Industrial Revolution after examining the statements of contemporaries.[47] On the basis of testimony presented to Parliament, the length of the working day, and actual factory rules prohibiting merriment of any sort, the deleterious effects of industrial capitalism are impossible to ignore.

In rural areas, where the spread of commercial agriculture threatened recreations by removing space for play, football matches occasionally served as vehicles of protest. The enclosure of open fields was one disruption of social relations which peasants protested with a football match. As livelihoods were jeopardized by enclosure and as the "straightforward nexus of wages ... bound the landless to the landed,"[48] the loss of recreational resources also was perceived. Symbolic protests against the fencing-off of open fields were undertaken in the guise of football matches, and peasants often gathered on the land that was to be enclosed and played football there until they were removed by force.

Some historians[49] have implied that enclosures benefited the entire village population. Yet the occurrence of football-enclosure riots, along with incendiarism, violations of game statutes, and the destruction of machinery demonstrate that there was strong opposition to the changes occurring in the countryside. A football-enclosure protest in Northamptonshire illustrates this point. Opponents of the enclosure at West Haddon placed an otherwise innocuous advertisement in the 29 July 1765 issue of the *Northhampton Mercury*, announcing a "Foot Ball Play" for 1 August. The *Mercury* of 5 August carried the results of the match: the players pulled up and burned the fences around the field and caused damage estimated at £1,500. They escaped capture by dragoons sent from Northampton when the purpose of the game became clear, and the next issue of the *Mercury* contained an offer of reward for information concerning the original football advertisement. In a September issue, the *Mercury* promised a £20 reward for the apprehension of Francis Botterill, a woolcomber, and John Fisher, a weaver, both accused of inserting the advertisement. Botterill and Fisher eluded the authorities.[50] The Holland Fen in Lincolnshire was the site of a similar demonstration in 1768, when more than two hundred people, objecting to an enclosure, began a game of football. After two hours, authorities arrived and committed some of the players to jail.[51]

However vigorous the protests might have been, the enclosures continued. The appropriation of common lands by large proprietors may have increased the value of their holdings: the expansion of the amount of land under cultivation provided food for towns and raw materials for industrialization. The livelihoods of the smaller proprietors were greatly changed, if not ruined, by the same process. Hobsbawm has speculated that even if enclosures and rationalized production in agriculture created more regular employment, they did not "compensate for the poor man's loss of independence."[52] The greater attention paid to market forces by large landowners stimulated a quest for efficiency that transformed many customs of rural England, and recreations were but one aspect of culture affected.

Many contemporaries ascribed the decline of football to enclosure. William Howitt maintained that football had "almost gone out of use with the enclosure of wastes and commons."[53] At Hornsea, after the enclosures of 1809, a chronicler observed that "football, which had been much practised up to that time, has necessarily been disused."[54] Enclosures at Pudsey, Ratby, Bicester, Portsmouth, and Coventry had the same effect. These instances and others that went unrecorded permitted Strutt to write in 1801 that football "seems to have fallen into disrepute, and is but little practised."[55] Strutt and other authors lamented the demise of preindustrial sports, and saw their demise as part of the decline of an England that was changing irrevocably. While rural life might not have been quite as idyllic as many writers implied, poems such as Goldsmith's "Deserted Village" (1770) did reflect basic social changes. A variety of sports and other amusements had constituted the charms of old village life, "but all these charms," according to Goldsmith, "are fled."[56]

Football was not a passing fancy, randomly played in one century and then less preferred in the next. Rather, the incidence of play was reduced by the actions of property owners who sought to improve the value of their holdings. By the middle of the nineteenth century, what one journalist called the spread of "true commercial principles" and improvements in farming had done "what Prynne and Prym could not effect." Country gentlemen accelerated the number of enclosure bills before Parliament, and village greens were reduced considerably or, in some cases, "swallowed up entire." The same journalist observed that

> one common right was ignored, the right of the people to the green playground where their rude forefathers had disported themselves, and the village lads and lasses were deprived of the ancestral turf where their parents and grandparents had made merry before them.[57]

Football players in the country as well as in the cities had less time, space, and energy for their game. Peter Bailey has argued that the industrial working class was not entirely without recreation during the early decades of the factory system. However, he noted a shift from "ritualised exercises of a traditional popular hedonism" to "formless and compulsive compensations for the strains of a coercive industrial society."[58] This shift is represented by the transition from outdoor, physical recreations to indoor activities which focused on the pub, although Bailey recognized the existence of rear guard battles to preserve the customs of an older England. While middle-class reformers looked askance at pub culture and attempted to provide "rational recreation" on occasion to the working class, the pub was more than a mere drinking hall. Glee clubs, bowling alleys, and libraries were among the diversions offered there. But while reformers were mistaken in their view of the pub as an immoral influence on workers, the amusements to be found there, however diverse, were fundamentally different from those of the preindustrial plebeian culture. The pub was no substitute for what that culture had provided to earlier generations.

Joseph Arch, the founder and leader of the National Agricultural Labourers' Union, recalled from his own childhood in the mid-nineteenth century that a village youth

> had two kinds of recreation open to him. He could take his choice between lounging and boozing in the public house, or playing bowls in the bowling alley. That was all. There were no cricket or football clubs, no Forester's meetings.[59]

William Pickford, an official of the Football Association at the turn of the twentieth century, remembered growing up in Little Lever, a village in

Lancashire. The town's inhabitants were employed primarily as coal miners, cotton mill operatives, or as workers in the bleaching and chemical works. In such an industrial area as this, people "lived hard and had little opportunity for recreation. . . . For us boys in the 1860s, there were no organized games. I never saw a cricket bat or footballl"[60]

These conditions were typical of those of other regions as well. The picture that emerges is one of a bleak, austere England that afforded little relief from the grind of a workday or week as basic social relations and working conditions were transformed. In 1840, Joseph Fletcher, an assistant hand-loom weaver commissioner for Coventry, testified before the Select Committee on the Health of Towns that the "want of open spaces applies to almost all the large towns." After stating that football had "greatly declined among young men," Fletcher was asked whether he found "generally that there is a want of active amusements among the labouring classes"; he acknowledged that such a void was "general among the manufacturing population."[61] Even in 1878, after reform legislation had increased leisure time for some workers,[62] W. Stanley Jevons noted that there were

> large parts of the manufacturing and more thickly populated districts of the kingdom where pure and rational recreation for the poorer classes can hardly be said to exist at all.[63]

Witnesses before other committees were moved to declare their own particular districts as the most deficient for working-class recreation. John Wardle, a cutler, asserted in 1843 that no manufacturing town

> is worse situated for places for public or healthful recreation than Sheffield. Thirty years ago it had numbers of places as common land where youths and men could have taken exercise at cricket, quoits, football, and other exercises. Scarce a foot of all these common wastes remain for the enjoyment of the industrial classes.[64]

R. H. Horne, a member of the Commission on Childrens Employment who reported for Wolverhamptom, observed that the working class had "no regular time whatever for healthful recreation; their only play-time is the hour allowed for dinner."[65] These findings were consistent with those of other commissioners. John Leifchild, for instance, correlated the amount of recreation time to the length of the workday and concluded that the three or four universally established holidays of the year were "of course observed," but

> in no case is any determinate time allotted for daily recreation. All that is enjoyed is obtained at the close of the day, in the passage from the works to the home, by such as have at that time strength or spirits for it.[66]

Ten years earlier, the parliamentary report on the state of public walks had stressed the paucity of recreational facilities for the working class:

> As respects those employed in the three great Manufactures of the Kingdom, Cotton, Woollen, and Hardware, creating annually an immense Property, no

provision has been made to afford them the means of healthy exercise or cheerful amusement with their families, on their Holidays or days of rest.[67]

Nineteenth-century Manchester frequently has been cited to illustrate disparities in wealth within one community, and the impoverishment of England's working class. It is appropriate to describe recreational opportunities in Manchester as a way of summarizing an element of working-class life during the first half century of industrialization. In Manchester, there were

> no public promenades, no avenues, no public gardens, and no public common. . . . Everything in the suburbs is closed against them; everything is private property; in the midst of the beautiful scenery of England the operatives are like the Israelites of old, with the promised land before them, but forbidden to enter it.[68]

While many traditional recreations, including football, were no longer enjoyed, as those who participated in them were transformed into wage workers, it appeared that football would die out altogether. It is hard to imagine that the rowdy plebeian game would prove useful to and experience a renaissance at England's prestigious public schools. Yet, it was in this environment that football was next accepted, although in a considerably modified way. Changes in the social profile of the participants and the radically different demands upon them affected the way in which new players in the early nineteenth century molded "football."

Football was first positively identified at a university in 1555, at St. John's College, Oxford, where it was banned. According to Magoun, the earliest recorded instance of football play at Cambridge was in 1574, when it was restricted by general order.[69] At both universities, the game closely resembled that played in the preindustrial village, and severe penalties, ranging from fines to expulsion, were incurred by those who played it. The statutes were repeatedly broken and rewritten, so that in 1636, the Oxford University Statutes specified that no scholars were to play football "within the University or its precincts (and particularly not in the public streets and places of the city) whether alone or by themselves or in the company of townsmen."[70]

The opposition to football at the universities is analogous to the disdain in which this plebeian sport was held in upper class society in general. Well into the nineteenth century Oxford and Cambridge were populated by the sons of the aristocracy and gentry, and it is therefore possible to ascribe patrician attitudes toward football to scholars at these institutions. Perhaps the game also displeased university administrators because it diverted scholars who, it was believed, should have devoted themselves entirely to their studies.

In spite of football's low reputation, the excitement of the game continued to appeal to young university men. Football attracted an even greater following at England's public schools where the perception of football as a game unfit for young gentlemen prevailed among educators. Even by 1831, when football had achieved considerable, although unsanctioned, popularity in the schools, its lower-class taint was a factor in its rejection by some. One Etonian considered football to be

> not at all gentlemanly. It is a game which the common people of Yorkshire are particularly partial to, the tips of their shoes being heavily shod with iron; and frequent death has been known to ensue from the severity of the blow inflicted thereby.[71]

Samuel Butler sought to restrict football at Shrewsbury, maintaining that the game was "more fit for farm boys and labourers than young gentlemen."[72]

But the schoolboys' urge to play football was undamped by such deprecations. As a consequence of the seemingly irrepressible attractions of football and its concomitant reputation as an uncouth pastime, educators assumed the task of modifying football to make it an acceptable, even beneficial, pastime for public school students. By the third and fourth decades of the nineteenth century, as a refined version of football evolved on the playing fields of the public schools, football as a working-class sport had declined because its former practitioners now lacked the necessary time and space for play. Football was becoming a pastime of the upper classes and was transformed in their image, as the game no longer resembled peasant-artisan brawls.

The same forces that contributed to the eclipse of plebeian football simultaneously elicited the need for an efficient and well-trained bureaucracy to direct a society that was growing more complex. "Booby squires" were caricatures that were tolerated in the eighteenth century, but for whom there was no room in an England where more and more members of the ruling class were influenced by new developments in industry and scientific farming. A greater awareness of price fluctuations, for instance, stimulated enclosures, while the growth of factories provided a wider scope for investment. Demand for raw materials, ranging from wool to iron ore, also strengthened connections between urban and rural entrepreneurs during the first decades of the Industrial Revolution. The composition and policies of England's ruling class were transformed, and new demands were made upon it.

As government policy came to reflect the needs and interests of the emerging middle class in matters as vital as parliamentary representation and laissez-faire, other aspects of life also were affected. The public schools, long a preserve of the preindustrial elite, were unregulated and lacked a well-defined educational purpose. Part of the reforming zeal of the middle class was aimed in their direction.[73]

Reformers challenged the public schools to prove their social worth. A nation which dominated world trade and which was experiencing rapid shifts in its social and political structures required intelligent administration, and this, according to the critics, was not being provided by the select public schools. Educational methods, the reformers argued, had to be overhauled to produce a bureaucracy and a political leadership that could understand and meet the needs of a complex, changing society.

Elie Halevy has described "middle class opposition" to a curriculum that emphasized Greek and Latin and devoted little time to studies pertaining to the new economic and technological realities. In 1815, critics decried public school education which was "devoid of every 'utilitarian' feature and [was] ill-adapted to the needs of a practical age."[74] Jeremy Benthan, in *Chrestomathia* (1816), proposed an alternative model of education "for the middle rank of life" who sought "useful and not merely ornamental instruction."[75] Prior to the publication of Bentham's work, according to Southwood Smith in the radical *Westminster Review*, there has been "no plan of instruction [for] those engaged in active business life," and nothing had been done to "enable those who are actually to conduct the affairs of the world."[76] Although educational methods were not recast to the degree recommended by Bentham, works such as *Chrestomathia* reflected middle-class dissatisfaction and helped to generate educational reform.

The honors and rewards accorded to tradition at the expense of merit were also criticized. Reformers pointed to aristocratic and gentry domination of the schools at a time when the wealth and influence of the industrial bourgeoisie was increasing. In the period 1800–1830 only eighty-six middle-class students were admitted to Rugby, and there was a declining rate of middle-class admissions after 1820. Norman Wymer has concluded that the middle classes were "anxious to give their sons a better education than they themselves had enjoyed," and therefore urged a revamping of the public schools in ways which would allow entree to their offspring.[77]

Such liberal educators as Thomas Arnold, the headmaster at Rugby from 1827–1842, responded with pervasive, innovative changes in academic, admissions, and extracurricular policies for public schools. Unlike previous headmasters, Arnold did not seek to extinguish or punish the exuberance of students whose boisterous behavior had been taken as evidence of academic failure by critics. Rather, he sought to direct the more rambunctious student activities to a loftier goal. Arnold's educational vision extended to the playing fields, and discipline, which was thought to encourage more serious academic pursuits, was introduced through a variety of devices, including the codification of football. By injecting a sense of organization and purpose into what had been an anarchic fray, Arnold at the same time instilled values which would be required of future generations of the ruling class.

Sports were legitimized in the public schools, and helped channel student energy constructively through athleticism which was "at once healthy and absorbing." Many otherwise disruptive schoolboys, according to Hon. Edward Lyttelton, were

> kept from the multifarious evils which flourish among the wholly idle. Diminish the power of athleticism, and vice is, so to speak, unfettered and turned loose."[78]

Football, one of the more popular outdoor games, was assigned an educative function. The use of football as a heuristic device was appreciated by educators, so that "when the new discipline was introduced in other schools, there went with it Rugby football."[79]

As football developed in the public schools after the 1830s, it was refined in order to serve as an educational tool appropriate for the upper classes. Rules evolved and individual codes were adopted at each school. The boundaries for play were established, matches were played for specific lengths of time, and certain actions were prohibited, depending on the particular code at such schools as Rugby, Eton, and Harrow. Organized tournaments between forms and houses within a school replaced more spontaneous and variegated play patterns, and reports of school matches appeared in middle-class sporting journals of London during the third quarter of the nineteenth century.[80]

A comparison of schoolboy football with its preindustrial predecessor demonstrates that game regulations and factors such as "competition" are socially determined and mutable. Given the flexible and irregular time and work patterns of preindustrial society, it would have been self-defeating to set the number of players for a match. Boundaries, too, had been subject to flux, partly because the contours of the countryside changed with the spread of commercial agriculture. More importantly, plebeian football had served little purpose beyond recreation: it was not organized to promote a disciplined elite and it was not designed to encourage traits among players which could one day benefit "the nation." Tournaments and competition had little importance, and players had no need to promulgate rules. The peasant-artisan games were extensions of village or town traditions, and football was only part of a larger celebration.

In contrast, Wellington's remark that the battle of Waterloo was won on the playing fields of Eton was amplified by adherents of schoolboy football. Modifications in educational policy were praised in part because of the way in which they facilitated the preparation of England's leaders. Writers lauded the use of sports and games by school administrators, as the children of the ruling class needed to develop skills that would enable them alternately to "command a division" and accept responsibilities for the "government of the nation." The education received on the playground was "of the highest value," and football in particular was

> so popular at all the leading schools at which are being trained and educated the youths from whose ranks the vacancies in the highest places in the country will, by and bye, have to be filled.[81]

In the first issue of *Bat and Ball*, which described itself as a "High-Class Weekly Journal of Football, Cricket, and Amateur Athletics," an editorial writer claimed that the

> proud boast that our Queen holds the sceptre of an empire on which the sun never sets, has been rendered possible by the discipline and training that our English lads have received in the cricket and football fields.[82]

In 1880, a writer noted that athletic activity was a part of the "education of the boys of our higher classes." Through sports such as football, the schoolboy acquired discipline by being

> raised to a post of command, where he feels the gravity of responsible office and the difficulty of making prompt decisions and securing willing obedience.[83]

By regulating behavior on the playing field, the schools distanced their new version of football from the plebeian variety. This enhanced the game's potential as a means for training a civil-service and military elite, and it also reenforced notions of class exclusiveness which had by no means been extinguished with industrialization.

When public school administrators modified football in the 1840s and 1850s, they were aware of the prejudices of older elites, who sought to preserve gentlemanly appearances, as well as the wishes of newer sections of the middle class, whose strivings for respectability would seem wasted if their sons engaged in uncouth free-for-alls. The new arrangements provided a distinct contrast to the anarchic brawls which had colored the perception of football through the early nineteenth century. Educators recognized the need for discipline and rationality suggested by the growing complexity of the period, and they realized that it was "impossible that the disorganized rowdyism of the ploughboys could be permitted in the well-disciplined schools."[84] Indeed, a writer for *The Field* observed in 1861 that students at Eton and Rugby would engage in sports "not participated in by the humbler classes."[85]

Despite different specifications, football appeared in all public schools as a well-controlled event, meeting the demands for consistency and purpose. The main divergences among the schools focused on the issue of whether carrying the ball (versus kicking it) was acceptable, and whether physical contact should be permitted. In a purely kicking game, less contact among players was allowed, and players could use their hands only for stopping or catching the ball. This version of the game was adopted by players at Harrow, where goals were scored by kicking the ball between posts, as there were no crossbars.

The Rugby game, also played at Marlborough and Cheltenham, was at the opposite end of the spectrum. After the kickoff, the offensive team proceeded upfield until the player carrying the ball was physically stopped. The ball was then either passed to a teammate or fought for in a scrummage. A goal was registered when the ball was kicked over the crossbar.

The Eton version was a mixture of the two styles. In it, there were only two occasions for physical contact—the bully, or initial scramble for possession, and the conversion attempt after the ball passed the opponent's end line. The Eton version fixed the number of players per side at eleven, and this number was accepted by the Football Association when it was formed in 1863.[86]

While disparities between individual school codes often seemed enormous to players of the 1860s, the existence of any code that was consistently applied and respected represented a significant step away from the plebeian game. Whether players regulated themselves or a referee was asked to officiate, a modicum of order was expected by schoolboy players at mid-century. An element of civility was also cultivated, so that even the Rugby game, the most physical of all public-school versions of football, came to possess its own etiquette. The roughest aspect of the game, hacking (kicking to the shins), was not always countenanced, as the following excerpt from *Tom Brown's School Days* indicates:

> "But why do you wear white trousers in November?" said Tom. He had been struck by this peculiarity in the costume of almost all the school-house boys. "Why bless us, don't you know? . . . Why, today's the school-house match. Our house plays the whole school at football. And we all wear white trousers, to show 'em we don't care for hacks."[87]

White pants stained from a hack could provide evidence of unsportsmanlike conduct, and such a uniform was one defense against fouling. Although hacking was retained by Rugbeians, the modern game of soccer as it was formulated by schoolboy players from Eton, Harrow, and other schools banned hacking and similar violence.

The physical contact permitted under the Rugby code discouraged numerous middle-class players, particularly those who had since graduated. As a journalist suggested in 1863, other codes were preferable to the regulations adopted by Rugbeians, whose style of football was

> hardly suited to the staid man of business, who could not afford for the sake of a Saturday afternoon's football match to give up two months of "the half" with a broken leg, or walk about the Temple or Capel-court limping from shin abrasions or other pleasantries incidental to "hacking and tripping."[88]

Gibson and Pickford observed that whichever code one wished to examine, the schoolboy game would prove to be altogether less violent when compared to peasant and artisan clashes. Violent elements that remained in school-boy football in the 1860s were isolated and criticized. While the name "football" had been given to both the plebeian and public-school versions of the sport, the authors concluded that the older game had "passed through the refining mill of the schools and was returned again in a new and worthier garb."[89] It is a moot point whether the game actually was "worthier." However, it certainly differed drastically from the peasant-artisan form that it had supplanted.

As the codification process continued at the public schools through the middle of the nineteenth century, generations of graduates who sought to play football found it increasingly difficult to organize matches. Disputes occurred when graduates of different schools met socially and considered playing football. An article in *Chambers Journal* illustrated the dilemma:

> We had gathered in a group in the centre of the ground, and the captains had tossed for choice of goals, when it was discovered that one of the players was

engaged in ingeniously affixing to the goal sticks a cross-bar about ten feet from the ground. "What rules are we to play by?" asked one on observing this. "Oh, Rugby, of course," answered two or three veterans of the "Old Bigside"; and simultaneously others cried "Eton" and "Harrow." It soon appeared probable that our match, which had held out such a charming prospect, would not be played at all. The Harrovians flatly declined to play if *shinning* and carrying the ball were to be allowed, declaring them both to be outrages upon the first principles of the game. The Rugbeians replied that they did not care for football without these features, and suggested that the Harrow game was only suited for little boys and girls. The Etonians thought football without *bullies* would be very slow and dull. As regarded shinning, they had had a little experience; they would prefer not to allow it, but if it came to a question of kicking legs, they could give and take as well as any Rugby player. Then the cross-bar was objected to—not that the other point had been settled—and there was a coalition between the Etonians and Harrovians against this "absurd innovation." . . . The ladies sent out to know why the game did not begin. We tried to play, leaving the question of rules for consideration at some other time, but our game soon broke down. Oil and water will mix as readily as the systems of football now practiced at Rugby, Eton, and Harrow.[90]

The author stated that the "decay" of football could be attributed to the "laws which regulate the game" and to the "wide differences existing between them at different schools."[91]

Other writers discussed how the differences among public-school codes made competition difficult for graduates. In an 1861 editorial, *The Field* asked, "what happens when a game of football is proposed at Christmas among a party of young men assembled from different schools?" As a call for a single, universal football code, the editor answered his own question: "Alas! We have seen the attempt made again and again, but invariably with failure as a result."[92] Two years later, *The Field* printed a ten-part series that described the various football rules which had evolved at the public schools and stressed the need for a codification conference, where an amalgamation of rules could occur.[93]

Bell's Life contained similar descriptions of the futile attempts of football play by graduates of one school who refused to alter elements of their code to accomodate equally stubborn old boys from other institutions. A contributor observed that "no two clubs played the same game in all points" and asserted that a single code "might bring all into harmonious working."[94] This was also the assessment of "Etonensis," whose letter appeared in the *Times:*

I am myself an Etonian, and the game of football as played by us differs essentially in most respects from that played at Westminster, Rugby, Harrow, and most other London clubs. Now, this difference prevents matches being made or played between either school or club; and, furthermore, prevents a player from gaining the credit of playing well anywhere but among his own associates. Now, sir, all these annoyances might be prevented by framing a set of rules for the game of football to be played everywhere. Say, the captains of the football elevens at Eton, Westminster, and Rugby, and the presidents of one or two London clubs meet, with members of either University, and frame the rules for one universal game.[95]

Attempts were already under way to codify football rules when this letter appeared. In 1862, J. C. Thring, a Shrewsbury and Cambridge graduate, formulated a ten-rule proposal to alleviate the problems faced by graduates. A committee was formed the following year to amplify Thring's proposals. Each committee member had played football at public school and was acquainted with the divergence of styles among the institutions. The committee members were:

R. H. Blake (Eton)	J. T. Prior (Marlborough)
W. T. Trench (Eton)	W. P. Crawley (Marlborough)
W. R. Collyer (Rugby)	H. L. Williams (Harrow)
W. T. Martin (Rugby)	W. S. Wright (Harrow)
Rev. R. Burn (Shrewsbury)	

The movement for a single football code which could be enjoyed by graduates of all public schools gained momentum. Letters and articles followed, and, finally, in the autumn of 1863, graduates of several schools met for the purpose of properly administering the game. At the meeting in London on 26 October, the chairman stated that it had been a longtime desire to form a set of rules which the London clubs should adopt among themselves, "as there were so many different ways of playing."[96] Various proposals for a single code were considered, and representatives from the schools were invited to participate in future discussions. However, representatives from Harrow, Eton, Winchester, Rugby, and Westminster refused to accept rules other than those which they themselves followed. They declined invitations to a meeting which was to finalize a body of standardized football rules, and the graduates proceeded without active public school players. On 24 November 1863, they founded the Football Association.

The Association was created to administer a game enjoyed almost exclusively by men and boys whose social profile fit the public-school mold. The backgrounds of the founders of the Football Association and the composition of the initial member teams (among whom were graduates of Harrow, Charterhouse, Kensington Grammar School, and Blackheath School) illustrate this point. The Association recruitment drive of 1869 was directed exclusively to upperclass, public-school participants, and by 1870 the Association's roster listed the following clubs:

Amateur Athletic	Forest School
Barnes	Holt
Bramham College	Hull College
Charterhouse	Hitchin
Clapham	Kensington School
Crowley (Oxford)	Leamington College
Crystal Palace	London Scottish Rifles
Donnington School	London Athletic

Milford College	Upton Park
No Names	Wanderers
Royal Engineers	Westminster
Reigate	West Brompton College
Sheffield (Old Harrovians)	Worlaybe House (Roehampton)
Totteridge Park	

Judging by the rise in Football Association membership, the game had grown in popularity during the 1860s among schoolboys and graduates. But there is no such exact way to measure the extent to which earlier, less formalized versions of football were retained in the schools. The schools had, by the early 1870s, adopted rules promulgated by the Football Association, and public-school graduates of the 1860s participated in matches that were sponsored by the organization. Etonians and Harrovians comprised teams that were particularly successful through the early 1880s in Football Association tournaments. The increasingly frequent mention of Association football in journals and newspapers at this time also suggests that the popularity of the standardized game was growing.

In 1871, the Football Association inaugurated its sponsorship of the Challenge Cup competition, a tournament to decide the team championship of organized football. All member clubs were invited to compete for the Cup in a tournament similar to public school "eliminations." Attendance at matches rose markedly with the initiation of Challenge Cup games, and the games received greater newspaper coverage. This augmented the prestige and power of the organization that regulated the matches, and the members of the Football Association Committee became more influential as football continued to attract a wider audience.

For the Football Association, that audience comprised men who had graduated from public schools. As athletic and sporting journals of the period attested, the majority of graduates had ample time and money for some form of recreational activity. The contributor to *Chambers Journal* had graduates in mind when he declared that sports refreshed those who were burdened by "sedentary occupations, excessive reading, and close application to business."[97] A writer in *The Field* stressed the benefits of football, particularly its potential for "counteracting the prejudicial results of continuous mental application of that kind which imposes sedentary habits." He added that the schools "collectively contain the vast body of football players" and that "most of the elder men who are patrons of the game learned it at these establishments."[98] The Wanderers of 1871, winners of the first Football Association Cup competition, illustrate this point. They included four Harrow graduates, three Etonians, and one representative each from Westminster, Charterhouse, Oxford, and Cambridge.

Football was played and governed by men whose amateur code was predicated upon their accessability to leisure resources. The amateurism of public-school graduates corresponded to their social and economic status; for them, football was the innocent diversion of the upper and middle classes who had no other thought than to pay for their own boots and clothes, take their own railway tickets, discharge their own hotel bills, or entertain the teams that visited them.[99]

Clearly, public school graduates needed little recompense for playing football.

The Football Association would not have to concern itself with distinctions between amateurism and professionalism for close to two decades. Football, as it developed in the middle of the nineteenth century, was an old-boy game which gravitated naturally toward amateur principles. C. W. Alcock, a Harrow graduate and the secretary of the Football Association from 1870 to 1895, recalled that up to 1884, the game had been "exclusively an amateur sport, and no doubt its founders never in their wildest dreams contemplated the possibility of such a figure as a professional."[100] However, shifts in the relative strengths and positions of classes in English society made the issue of professionalism the overwhelming concern of the Football Association between 1880 and 1885. The outcome of the controversy over professionalism would again radically alter the nature of football.

Notes

1.   Francis Magoun's "The History of Football from the Beginnings to 1871," contains the most numerous descriptions of preindustrial football. Morris Marples drew extensively from Magoun's examples and included others in *A History of Football* (London: Secker and Warburg, 1954).

2.   Dennis Brailsford, in *Sport and Society: Elizabeth to Anne* (London: Routledge and Keegan Paul, 1969), and Robert Malcolmson, in *Popular Recreations in English Society 1700–1850* (Cambridge: Cambridge University Press, 1973) look to prevailing societal factors to explain the features and functions of sports and other pastimes in preindustrial England.

3.   Edward P. Thompson, "Time, Work-Discipline and Industrial Capitalism," *Past and Present* (December 1967), p. 80.

4.   J. H. Plumb, *The Commercialization of Leisure in Eighteenth Century England* (Reading: University of Reading, 1973), p. 18 n.

5.   Peter Burke, *Popular Culture in Early Modern Europe* (London: Maurice Temple Smith, 1978), pp. 277–278.

6.   Strutt, *Sports and Pastimes*, p. xxv.

7.   Ibid., pp. 85, 62.

8.   Ibid., pp. 93–94.

9.   John Strype, *A Survey of the Cities of London and Westminster* (London: 1720), I:301.

10.   Magoun, "The History of Football," p. 40.

11.   Beatrice White, ed., *The Eclogues of Alexander Barclay* (London: E.E.T.S., 1928), 175:184.

12.   George Thorn-Drury, ed. *The Poems of Edmund Waller* (London: Lawrence and Bullen, 1893), p. 3.

13.   *Worchestershire County Records,* Div. I (Calendar of Quarter Sessions, Worcester, 1900), I 497–498; and J. C. Jeaffreson, ed. *Middlesex County Records* (London: Middlesex County Record Society, 1886), p. 97.

14. Cf. *The Field* (London), 24 October 1863, p. 414, for a description of football among Warwickshire miners; and W. Carew Hazlitt, *Faiths and Folklore* (London: Reeves and Turner), I:245 for "northern colliers."

15. John Gay, *Trivia, Or the Art of Walking the Streets of London,* W. H. Williams, ed. (London: Daniel O'Connor, 1922), p. 23; and Marples, *A History of Football,* pp. 19, 80.

16. Malcolmson, *Popular Recreations,* chapter two.

17. Magoun, "The History of Football," pp. 99–138. Magoun referred to drapers, quarriers, and shoemakers along with agricultural laborers who played football on Shrove Tuesday. Before one match, the mayor of Derby threatened players with court action for the "breaking of Windows and doing other mischief to the Person and Properties of the Inhabitants." [p. 112.]

18. *Lacedemonian Mercury* (London), 18 March 1692, p. 2.

19. Marples, *A History of Football,* p. 58.

20. Brailsford, *Sport and Society,* pp. 198–199.

21. Malcolmson, *Popular Recreations*, p. 13.

22. Thompson, "Time, Work-Discipline and Industrial Capitalism," pp. 70–79.

23. David Murray, *Early Burgh Organization in Scotland* (Glasgow: Maclehose, Jackson and Co., 1924), I:223.

24. "Diary of Jacob Bee of Durham" in *Six North Country Diaries,* John Hodgson Crawford, ed. (Durham: Andrews and Co., 1910), p. 47.

25. Elyot's remarks on football can be found in *Faiths and Folklore,* p. 243, and Stubbes' denunciation of 1583 was contained in his *Anatomy of Abuses* (London: New Shakespeare Society, 1879), ser. VI, no. 6, I:184.

26. William Hutton, *The History of Derby* (London: Nicholson and Bentley, 1817), p. 184.

27. The consistency of preindustrial, plebeian football has prompted Eric Dunning to formulate fourteen general structural-functional properties for this version of the game. See "Industrialization and the Incipient Modernization of Football," *Arena,* no. 1 (1975), pp. 103–111.

28. MacGregor, *Pastimes and Players,* p. 94.

29. *The Times,* (London), 6 March 1840, p. 6.

30. Ralph Strauss, *The London Spy Compleat, by Ned Ward* (London: Folio Society, 1955), p. 230.

31. Cf. Brailsford, *Sport and Society*, pp. 71–72.

32. L. A. Govett, *The King's Book of Sports* (London: Elliot Stock, 1890), pp. 38–39.

33. Ibid., p. 37.

34. Hazlitt, *Faiths and Folklore,* p. 244.

35. Stephen Glover, *The History of the County of Derby* (Derby: Henry Mozley, 1829), I:310.

36. MacGregor, *Pastimes and Players,* p. 99.

37. G. M. Trevelyan, *English Social History* (London: Longman's, Green & Co., 1946), pp. 352–353.

38. G. M. Trevelyan, *History of England* (London: Longman's, Green & Co., 1947), p. 514.

39. Cf. Edward P. Thompson, "Patrician Society, Plebeian Culture," *Journal of Social History* (Summer 1974), p. 389; and Malcolmson, *Popular Recreations*, chap. 4.

40. Cf. Malcolmson, *Popular Recreations*, chap. 7.

41. Magoun, "The History of Football," p. 114.

42. Malcolmson, *Popular Recreations*, chap. 7.

43. Select Parliamentary Committee on Walks, *Parliamentary Papers,* 1833, vol. XV, p. 3.

44. Ibid., p. 55.

45. Douglas Reid, "The Decline of Saint Monday 1766–1876," *Past and Present* (May 1976), p. 84.

46. M. A. Bienefeld, *Working Hours in British Industry* (London, Wiedenfeld & Nicolson, 1972), p. 80.

47. See, for instance, the Factory Commission Reports of 1833, 1842, and 1843, which were among the many descriptions of factory conditions that came to the attention of Parliament.

48. Eric Hobsbawm and George Rude, *Captain Swing* (New York: Pantheon, 1968), p. 37.

49. J. D. Chambers and G. E. Mingay minimized the size of a rural proletariat created through enclosure and suggested that the number of smallholders increased; presumably, many landlords left tenants undisturbed. Chambers and Mingay conceded, however, that "access to commons and waste may have played an important prop in the economy of many cottagers" and that the removal of this prop was "undoubtedly a factor in the increasing poverty which characterized much of the countryside in the later eighteenth century and after." [*The Agricultural Revolution* (New York: Schocken, 1967).]

50. "An Eighteenth Century Inclosure and Football Play at West Haddon," *Northamptonshire Past and Present* (1968/1969), pp. 175–178.

51. W. Marrat, *The History of Lincolnshire, Topographical, Historical, and Descriptive* (Boston: published by the author, 1814), I:140–141.

52. Hobsbawm and Rude, *Captain Swing*, p. 35.

53. William Howitt, *The Rural Life of England* (London: Longman's, 1840), p. 527.

54. E. W. Bedell, *An Account of Hornsea* (Hull: 1848), p. 88.ʼ

55. Strutt, *Sports and Pastimes*, pp. 93–94.

56. Oliver Goldsmith, *Poetical Works* (Oxford: 1927), pp. 23–24.

57. *Chambers Journal,* 10 December 1864, p. 799.

58. Peter Bailey, *Leisure and Class in Victorian England: Rational Recreation and the Contest for Control, 1830–1885* (London: Routledge & Kegan Paul, 1978), p. 8.

59. Joseph Arch, *The Story of His Life, Told by Himself* (London, 1898), p. 34.

60. William Pickford, *A Few Recollections of Sport* (London: Football Association), p. 7.

61. Select Committee on the Health of the Towns, *Parliamentary Papers,* 1840, vol. XI, p. 70.

62. See Chapter Two: "The Basis for Professionalism."

63. W. Stanley Jevons, "Amusements of the People" *Contemporary Review* (London, October 1878), p. 499.

64. Report from Commissioners, Childrens Employment Commission, *Parliamentary Papers,* 1843, vol. XIV, p. E 23.

65. Ibid., vol. XV, p. Q 9.

66. Ibid., vol. XV, p. L 5–6.

67. Select Parliamentary Committee on Walks, *Parliamentary Papers*, 1833, vol. XV, pp. 4–5.

68. Leon Faucher, *Etudes sur l'Angleterre* (1845). [Cited in J. L. Hammond, "The Growth of Common Enjoyment," (London: Oxford University Press, 1933), p. 5.]

69. Magoun, "The History of Football," p. 73.

70. *Oxford University Statutes* (London, 1845), I:161.

71. H. J. C. Blake, *Reminiscences of Eton by an Etonian,* (Chichester, 1831), p. 47.

72. Cited in Eric Dunning, "Industrialization and the Incipient Modernization of Football," *Arena* (1975), p. 113.

73. In his section on public schools, R. K. Webb noted institutional developments "on which middle class attitudes, confidence, and power could rest, to survive with increasing strength." [*Modern England* (New York: Dodd, Mead and Co., 1971), p. 298.]

74. Elie Halevy, *A History of the English People in the Nineteenth Century: England in 1815* (New York: Barnes & Noble, 1968), p. 535.

75.   Jeremy Bentham, *The Works of Jeremy Bentham,* ed. John Bowring, (London, Simpkin & Marshall, 1843), VIII, *Chrestomathia,* p. 17.

76.   *Westminster Review,* (January, 1824), p. 45.

77.   Norman Wymer, *Dr. Arnold of Rugby* (London: Robert Hale, Ltd., 1953), p. 94.

78.   Hon. Edward Lyttelton, "Athletics in Public Schools," *Nineteenth Century* (London), January 1880, p. 50.

79.   T. W. Bamford, *Thomas Arnold* (London: Cresset Press, 1960), p. 188.

80.   See *Sporting Life, Bell's Life in London and Sporting Chronicle,* and *The Field* for this period.

81.   *The Field* (London), 24 Oct. 1863, pp. 413–414.

82.   *Bat and Ball* (Manchester), 13 September 1882, p. 1.

83.   Lyttelton, "Athletics in Public Schools," p. 44.

84.   Pickford and Gibson, *Association Football,* p. 20.

85.   *The Field,* 14 Dec. 1861, p. 525.

86.   *The Field* printed a ten-week serialized article in 1863 which described various school codes. An article in *Chambers Journal* (12 March 1864) also explained the rules of football as they developed in the public schools.

87.   Thomas Hughes, *Tom Brown's School Days* (New York: Macmillan, 1910), p. 96.

88.   *Bell's Life* (London), 12 Dec. 1863, p. 3.

89.   Pickford and Gibson, *Association Football,* p. 32.

90.   *Chambers Journal* (12 March 1864), p. 174.

91.   Ibid.

92.   *The Field,* 14 Dec. 1861, p. 525.

93.   *The Field,* 24 Oct. 1863 et. seq.

94.   *Bell's Life,* 12 Dec. 1863, p. 3.

95.   *The Times* (London), 5 Oct. 1863, p. 8.

96.   *Bell's Life,* 31 Oct. 1863, p. 2 (supplement).

97.   *Chambers Journal,* 12 March 1864, p. 174.

98.   *The Field,* 19 December 1863, p. 603.

99.   J. A. H. Catton, *The Real Football* (London: Sands & Co., 1900), p. 52.

100.   C. W. Alcock, "Association Football," *English Illustrated Magazine* (Jan. 1891), p. 285.

CHAPTER TWO

The Basis for Professionalism

The controversy over amateurism is centuries old.[1] Its advocates have glorified the purity of the amateur game and the strength of character that such competition is said to engender, and they have contrasted the amateur ideal of enjoying sports for its own sake to the more sordid, self-interested, and therefore less-enobling professional variety of athletic competition.

Johan Huizinga and Paul Weiss have participated in the debate over amateurism, and they, like many others who seek a pure realm for sports, have denigrated professionalism. Weiss has stated that compared to "true" amateurs, professionals are "better machines" but "not usually better human beings."[2] Scholars generally have agreed that professionalism has changed sports, but to understand the nature of this change, the focus must shift from morals and values to the process by which sports have been altered by the advent of professionalism.

An analysis of the professionalism controversy which raged in the early 1880s in English soccer contributes to an understanding of this process. In spite of the space devoted in the contemporary press to the purely moral benefits of amateurism, such benefits as were derived were likely speculative and impressionistic and not subject to historical proof. It is possible that moral benefits might have accrued to players and society at large from participation in amateur football; yet, despite that, we know that professionalism evolved and flourished. The reasons for the rise of professionalism in the face of such disapprobation are the concern here.

When C. W. Alcock, the secretary of the Football Association, stated that the Association's founders "never in their wildest dreams contemplated the possibility of such a figure as a professional,"[3] he was enunciating a position rooted in a mid-century reality. Before the 1870s, football was a casual pastime for schoolboys and wealthy sportsmen who had embraced an amateur code. There was little motivation for well-to-do public school graduates to assume careers as professional athletes; moreover, there was no demand for professional players. While football gained popularity as an organized gentleman's sport, there is no evidence in newspapers or Football Association records which would indicate working-class participation even on a small scale in the amateur game.[4]

As discussed earlier, industrialization and enclosure meant that significant sections of the working class enjoyed few outdoor sports during the first two thirds of the nineteenth century. The process of industrialization, which had engendered radical shifts in plebeian leisure and recreation, simultaneously facilitated the growth of large units of production at which huge numbers of workers were employed. The social and economic consequences of this development often involved a painful transformation of cottage workers and artisans into mill or factory hands, as their bargaining power and occupational distinctions were eroded with the simplification of the work routine. Yet the centralization of production and labor also would eventually provide workers with opportunities for concerted action in order to defend or improve their collective situation. The increased size and uniformity of the industrial working class were significant factors in English politics and labor relations after the initial shocks of proletarianization had been absorbed.

By the 1860s, and with increasing success in the following decade, rank-and-file militancy was instrumental in shortening the working day and week. Trade unions campaigned successfully for a nine-hour day with a shortened Saturday. (Previously, the working day in most trades extended from 6 A.M. to 6 P.M.). The better organized and more restrictive unions, such as those for skilled building trades workers, enjoyed the short Saturday, but such concessions had been obtained only after considerable struggle around mid-century, and only in a handful of occupations. London bricklayers, for instance, were granted a "four o'clock Saturday" in 1851 after a sixteen-week strike. Until well into the 1860s, the short Saturday was a rarity for most working people.

The growth of the trade union movement was, according to M. A. Bienefeld, a precondition for the success of the Nine Hours Movement of the early 1870s. Often, the demand for hours reform fostered the creation of militant unions, as broad sections of the working class closed down several branches of trade in pursuit of the shorter day. By 1875, the scope of reform was so extensive that participants in these disputes could "be said to have radically altered the country's perception of what constitutes a work day."[5] The "normal week" by this time was fifty-four to fifty-six and one-half hours, the nine-hour day had replaced the ten-hour shift, and the short Saturday was introduced in a number of industries.

The impact of the Nine Hours Movement on working-class leisure activities has been measured by Denis Molyneux, who focused on Birmingham. As a result of hours legislation and the new contractual agreements between workers and employers, the industrial working class was "better able, both physically and mentally, to consider making use of their leisure."[6]

Before 1871, regular physical recreation had been enjoyed only by a small section of the community, drawn "mainly from the upper and middle classes of Birmingham society."[7] Molyneux cited the lack of public recreation facilities prior to 1870 and the exclusiveness of athletic organizations. The Birmingham Athletic Club, one of the only such clubs in the city, described itself as "almost entirely composed of young Professional and Mercantile Men." Elsewhere, the Amateur Athletic Club formed in 1866 defined an "amateur" as someone who was not a mechanic, artisan, or laborer, and the Amateur Rowing Association and the Bicycle Union banned workingmen from membership.[8]

Molyneux observed a high correlation between the increase in leisure time in 1871–1872 and the expansion of physical recreation in the following twenty years.[9] The working class began participating in a number of sports, including cricket, cross-country running, swimming, cycling, tennis, and boxing; eight roller-skating rinks were opened in Birmingham alone between 1875 and 1877. A Birmingham alderman stated at a local Football Association dinner that he was "glad that within recent years artisans had taken such an interest in out-door games, especially on that weekly half-holiday, every Saturday."[10]

The spread of outdoor activities with the expansion of working-class leisure time and the rise of real wages stands in sharp contrast to the decline in physical activities and the reliance on the pub as a center for recreation that characterized the early decades of the Industrial Revolution. As leisure time and spendable incomes increased, working-class families were better able to take railway excursions (especially to the seaside) and to enjoy such other leisure pursuits as an afternoon at the races or an evening at the music hall.[11]

Journalists expressed particular interest in the increased participation in football. In 1880, the *Birmingham Daily Mail* reported that the progress of football during the past few years was "little less than marvelous." In 1874, participants in Association football had been "very few, and the clubs could have been counted on one's hand." By 1880, however, it was a "common occurrence for seventy or more legitimate matches to be played on Saturday."[12] By 1885, a writer ventured that "never in the memory of man . . . has any game attained such a wonderful popularity, and the public interest, instead of waning, grows stronger year by year."[13] A reporter for the *Midland Athletic Star* maintained that the "annals of British sports and pastimes present no case at all approaching the growth of Association football in popular favour," and he added that apart from the Midlands, only Lancashire had experienced a more dramatic acceptance of the game.[14] In Lancashire, the football mania among the working population was often discussed, and one writer for the *Preston Guardian* observed that "on every vacant piece of land can be seen the schoolboy and operative giving an exposition of its rules."[15]

Football always had the advantage of requiring little in the way of expensive equipment. A ball, or a reasonable facsimile (e.g., rags rolled tightly together) often was the only equipment absolutely necessary for a match. Aside from those expenses related to competition, such as the cost of uniforms and travel, the schoolboy version of the game cost no more to play than had the peasant-artisan variety. For this reason, football was an obvious recreational possibility for the millions of workers who had recently won shorter working hours. This was evident to sports reporters, who pointed out that football was

> within everyone's reach. The poorest lot of factory lads and the children of the humblest parents, when banded together into a club, can always obtain the wherewithal with which to purchase a ball and a pair of goal posts.[16]

The increase in football play in the late 1870s and early 1880s occurred more than five years after the expansion of working-class leisure time. Molyneux accounted for this lag in the popularization of the game by suggesting that it had to be reintroduced to the working class, and that a common code of play had to be accepted by the new participants. Such a code was often brought to a local district by returning public school graduates, as seems to have been the case in Darwen.[17] However, evidence to document the direct transmission of the game from former schoolboys to the working class is too sketchy to allow for the reconstruction of a clear picture of this process. This further supports the hypothesis that plebeian football had disappeared during the previous few decades. Adherents of the plebeian version presumably would have returned to it had it not been discouraged as industrialization spread.

The new working-class preference for an organized, codified form of football is both problematic and significant. Much can be inferred but little proven conclusively in an analysis of this trend. Could the adoption of the public-school game have demonstrated a vague extension of social control, wherein a specific code and ethos of play were formulated at the upper echelons of society and transmitted downward? Were bourgeois requirements for order now internalized by workers? Peter Bailey, among others, has stressed the way in which organized games served as "powerful instrument[s] for commanding social conformity, with a unique role to play in counteracting such divisive forces as class and race."[18] What is certain is that workers now embraced an organized and disciplined version of football.

That the working class preferred codified, Association football in the 1870s, just a few years after the ruling classes had made their momentous "leap in the dark" by extending the suffrage in 1867, makes the issue of control all the more pertinent. The transformation in outlook of the working-class leadership during the two previous decades provides a useful framework within which internal and imposed restraints on working-class militancy can be analyzed. John Foster has shown that working-class leaders often joined organizations dominated by the middle class that espoused the values and objectives of the bourgeoisie. As exposure to and assimilation within these groups enhanced the "cultural control" of the bourgeoisie, the working-class leadership rejected a more radical outlook which had prevailed earlier.[19] A relatively small group who were highly placed in adult education institutes, temperance societies, and cooperative movements functioned within the "cultural orbit of the bourgeoisie."[20]

If the proletarian leadership was influenced by middle-class institutions and was imbued with values which supported the status quo, other segments of the working class had not yet definitively embraced the social order recommended by their betters. The increase of leisure time created what might be termed a crisis of social control. Hours legislation expanded a "domain of free choice" in which workers could engage in personal pursuits. Such free choice could encourage ideas and movements hostile to the present regime, while the "corruption of leisure," according to Bailey, threatened to "undo the painstakingly fashioned bonds of a new work discipline in the labour force."[21]

It is within this context that the introduction of organized games into working-class culture occurred. W. Stanley Jevons bemoaned in 1878 the fact that working people seemed to have "forgotten how to amuse themselves." An excursion into the country, with no provision for music or harmless games, degenerated into "horse-play and senseless vulgarity; and . . . it is not surprising that the refreshment-bar and the nearest tap room are the chief objects of attention."[22]

Within a few years, the void in organized working-class leisure which Jevons decried would be filled by new recreational activities which were accompanied by distinct notions of proper behavior. Walvin has cited a variety of institutions such as churches and schools wherein the notion of "playing by the rules" was stressed.[23] Although no single causative factor can be isolated, the introduction to the working class of a codified form of football bears a striking similarity to the process which Foster associated with changes that occurred in education, temperance activities, and elsewhere in working-class life.

By the 1870s, neither the time nor the space necessary for the older plebeian version of football was available. Clearly, however, members of the industrial working class did possess by this date sufficient time to play as well as to watch a game that was better defined and more uniform than the versions of football which their forebears had played prior to industrialization. By the 1880s, well-financed football clubs replicated and normalized contemporary commercial-societal relationships and offered controlled sporting entertainment to paying spectators by the thousands.

On first glance, it would appear that by the 1880s football was becoming a truly national game. Molyneux listed twenty-four clubs in Birmingham in 1876–1877. Three years later, the number of clubs reached one hundred fifty-five. A variety of institutions—churches, the YMCA, factories, trade unions, and schools—sponsored football teams during the 1870s and early 1880s, and the sporting press of Lancashire and the Midlands in particular reported the matches and scores of these teams. It is possible to trace some of the prominent teams of a later period to the rather informal squads that appeared as football took hold. The Aston Villa F.C., for instance, began as the winter pastime of the Villa Cross Wesleyan Chapel congregation. Workers on the Lancashire and Yorkshire Railway founded the Newton Heath F.C.. which later became known as Manchester United. In the textile town of Blackburn, the local grammer school organized a team which, by the early 1880s, was renamed the Blackburn Rovers F.C. The popularity of football among working-class youth was reflected in the enthusiasm that surrounded local schoolboy football tournaments. *The Athlete* noted that boys who sometimes left school and went to work well before graduation were induced to return to school in order to compete in their football matches, only to leave for work once again when the competition was terminated.[24]

As the English working class rediscovered the game, football came to exist on at least two distinct levels. It continued to flourish as a casual pastime, played by ever-increasing numbers, and it also developed on a commercial, professional plane. Both facets of football's growth are basic to its history, and the latter trend certainly drew its sustenance from the grass-roots acceptance of the sport. Indeed, just as the professional game has expanded far beyond its dimensions of the 1880s, so has the informal, semiorganized variety been embraced as the national sport for close to a century. The presence of football play in virtually every park and recreation area since its reintroduction during the last quarter of the nineteenth century requires no further elaboration.

The social historian can glean a significant understanding of informal working-class recreation by looking at football as it was played fairly spontaneously in parks and sometimes even on city thoroughfares.[25] Yet while casual, amateur footballers substantially outnumbered those who played for their livelihood, the numerical dimension alone can be misleading. The emergence of football as a professional game comprised not only the development of a business structure but also its rapid growth as a spectator sport. The popular enthusiasm for watching professional football in some respects eclipsed mass participation in the sport, prompting J. E. Raphael of Oxford to state that

> Association is now played only by professional teams. In using the word "only" I am thinking of football from the spectator's standpoint, and although there may be, and doubtless are, a fair number of amateur "soccer" games being played every week, the man in the street seldom gives such matches a second thought. He wants to see a professional side, because he thinks he will get more for his money.[26]

The focus of this book from this point forward is on the growth of professional football.

The professional game reflected English society in the critical area of labor relations. Working-class fans could follow both the on-the-field heroics and the player-director struggles of their favorite teams. The clubs in the Football League received particularly wide coverage in the sporting press. The relationship of club directors to players and the relationship which existed among spectators and clubs are aspects of the social history of the period. Before analyzing these themes, it is useful first to discuss the commercial structure that arose in professional football.

If "time was money" to the eighteenth-century entrepreneur, the late-nineteenth-century businessman, observing the increase in leisure time within the industrial working class, came to realize that "free time was money." With the acceptance of the half-day Saturday and the formation of new patterns of leisure among millions who previously had not enjoyed much recreational activity, the leisure business found a basis for development. As money replaced tradition and birth as a medium for social intercourse, so too were recreations commercialized in the 1880s.

Football was by no means the only, or even the first, pastime to be affected in this manner. Wray Vamplew has contrasted annual one-day celebrations which included horse races to which no admission fee was charged to planned racing meets of the late nineteenth century which required an admission fee. The latter races offered little of the carnival atmosphere of the races of earlier days, and the jockeys participating in them were professional employees.[27] A writer in the *Birmingham Daily Mail* attacked the commercialization of track meets in terms which would shortly be applied to football: entrepreneurs held out cash prizes to insure an exciting tournament and, ultimately, a sizable gate. As a result, a "sordid tone" was given to "what ought to be a contest waged simply for the honour of the thing." A competition without the "mercenary cracks," concluded the writer, "would do athletics far more real good, although the 'gate' would not yield such a profitable result."[28] A cyclist, disgusted by the encroachment of professionals in his sport, was inspired to vent his feelings in verse:

> Talk to me of riding for fees!
> I scorn the mere thought of reward;
> In virtue this amateur sees
> All he aims at; he does, on my word.

> True nobility's knocked off the track
> By these riders for base L. S. D.*
> Who toil and keep muscle on rack
> Till they're worn out and then all's U. P.[29]

As entrepreneurs perceived the commercial potential of leisure time, they discovered that recreation could be marketed and sold. Consumers who had been denied traditional recreations for decades now sought some form of amusement for their Saturday afternoons. For a price, they could be entertained, and forms of entertainment such as horse racing and track meets were developed to satisfy and further the demand.

Yet, the providing of entertainment also had its costs, and a rational, businesslike mentality emerged as entrepreneurs replicated commercial relationships and techniques in the entertainment business. It soon became apparent that this trend brought with it certain built-in problems regarding contemporary attitudes toward recreation. There was hardly room for amateurism in sports if businessmen were to realize the commercial potential of their new trade.

*A reference to the monetary system (pounds, shillings, pence).

The features of the new version of football made the game a more attractive and marketable product. While the plebeian game had often included entire villages, various school codes had long since reduced the number of players for a match. By 1863, the Football Association had fixed the number of men per side at eleven, and the wide acceptance of Association rules eliminated mass participation in a single match. Similarly, during the first two-thirds of the nineteenth century, time and space allotted for football matches were standardized, making the game easier to follow. While peasants and artisans had played for as much time as it took to score a goal over a field that could be miles long, the modern version of football was played for a specified time on smaller grounds with clearly defined boundaries.

The limiting of the number of players per side had as an obvious consequence the creation of a separation between players and spectators. In mid-century, play space, whether public or private, had been monopolized by a handful of old boys, and spectators at their rather casual football games usually consisted of wives and schoolmates. In earlier versions of football, where there were no restrictions on the number of players per side, the primary participation was in playing the game. Once the number of players was limited, "participation" frequently was reduced to rooting for one team or another by onlookers who might have been active players in prior decades.

If a game could be played for a limited time on limited space, the question of who played would be decided according to skill: the best players performed while the less skilled sat, or went elsewhere. The increased publicity surrounding football usually lured nonplayers to stay and watch. Those who played had the opportunity to develop their skills even further, and players were perceived as men set apart by virtue of their athletic abilities. Growing numbers of people wanted to see them perform. This was noted by a writer for the *Midland Athletic Star* who, in 1882, correlated a "rapid growth of the game" and a

> proportionate eagerness of witnessing play of the highest order and excellence. As the players themselves become educated in the intricacies of passing, dodging, and combination . . . so do the thousands, who weekly cull enjoyment from witnessing a good game, become more and more appreciative of good play.[30]

In addition to a growing aesthetic appreciation of matches on the part of spectators, limited recreational resources perhaps inadvertently fostered the tendency to watch football. The expansion of public facilities for football in Birmingham, for instance, was steady after the 1870s. Yet, it took decades to provide adequate resources for the working population, in spite of the efforts of organizations such as the Open Space Movement, which emphasized the "common man's need for healthy outdoor sports" and which simultaneously deplored the "chronic shortage of playing room in the towns."[31] In 1887, the Baths and Parks Commission of Birmingham determined to close public parks to football players. *Sports and Play,* a Birmingham weekly, was quick to note that this "is so entirely a workingman's question that it behoves us all to strive hard" to have the ban rescinded. The *Sports and Play* editorial also mentioned that most footballers could not

> afford private grounds, and their only resource is the street. . . . Driven upon the streets, as these working boys and youths inevitably would be, what can be expected? They would in many cases be summoned and fined for obstruction and nuisance, and from that would spring a life of crime.[32]

Similar circumstances existed in other parts of the country. In Lancashire, there were complaints of football play in the streets of various towns in the 1880s, seemingly due to the lack of playground space. In Padihan, eight boys were brought before the town superintendant for making a thoroughfare "almost impassable" and were "severely cautioned" and fined 5 s. each, plus costs. Five other boys were summoned for committing the same offense at Higham.[33] In 1891, C. W. Alcock decried the lack of space for cricket and football in London, while the problem persisted in other regions for decades. In 1909, the *Derby Football Express* stated the matter succinctly: "there are not sufficient grounds for us all to play."[34]

The combination of an appreciation of the footballer's art and restricted space for mass participation created an audience for football matches. After 1880, large numbers of working people were anxious to attend games and were willing to pay for such entertainment. Sensing the possibilities for profit, entrepreneurs invested in football grounds, players, and all the paraphernalia necessary to field a team and provide a modicum of facilities for spectators. There was little question that spectators would pay to view the game, while entrepreneurs retained the receipts. This relationship obtained in football, horse racing, track meets, and other recreations, and it mirrored the contemporary form of commodity sales.

There was sufficient reason for optimism regarding the financial prospects for football. The enthusiasm of the working class for watching the game seemed unbounded, as illustrated in their support of football teams in Lancashire. The Darwen–Blackburn Rover match of 18 March 1882, was one of many which created the type of excitement that prompted increased investment. In view of the "large crowd to keep in hand," the Darwen committee strengthened pitch boundaries with extra posts and created additional entrances to the ground "for the great quantity of spectators expected." Nevertheless, a "tremendous crowd of spectators poured onto the field at least an hour and a half before the time advertised for the game to commence," and finally it was estimated that close to 20,000 people had purchased tickets for the match.[35]

Such enthusiasm extended to a group of female mill workers from Darwen who attended the game. One declared that she

> "wouldn't ceare heaw long we had to work short time if we could nobbut lick t'Rovers today," and there was a general response from her friends, "Me noather."[36]

Blackburn's victory no doubt disappointed the factory women but delighted Rover supporters. The latter planned to journey to London with their team, taking advantage of railroads, an increasingly important factor in the display of football talent and the transportation of spectators.[37] Working-class football fans in Blackburn also were prepared to forego a day's work in order to cheer for the Rovers, and over one thousand Blackburn supporters traveled to London to witness the Cup final in 1882. Prior to the day of the match, a factory owner in Blackburn promised to stop his mill "for the purpose of letting such of his workpeople as may feel disposed" follow the Rovers to London.[38]

Newspaper reports of football crowds in the early 1880s frequently described their size, enthusiasm, and seemingly insatiable demand for football. One writer speculated that if the 1882 Association Cup final were played in South Lancashire, rather than in London, "no football ground in the neighbourhood could have accomodated the numbers that would have clamoured for admission."[39] In Birmingham and in other parts of the Midlands, the picture was the same. Reporting from a Birmingham–Scotland match in March, 1882, a journalist stated that the

> enormous crowd was an imposing sight; they were closely packed all round the enclosure, the grandstands were full to repletion, and vehicles of all descriptions lined the track which circles the meadow. A small regiment of venturesome youths had perched themselves upon the two sheds . . . and all the persuasive eloquence of several policemen, and even stronger argument in the shape of a hose, failed to induce them to descend from their position. . . . The trees, and even shrubs, too, were taken advantage of by hundreds of juveniles, perched in mid-air like so many crows overlooking a field.[40]

At the same time, the levy of admission fees at matches revolutionized numerous aspects of football. The sport became less a gentleman's pastime and more a commercial enterprise when played at its highest levels. Relationships among teams increasingly came to resemble the relationships among ordinary competitive business firms. Indeed, the debate over professionalism was a by-product of the commercialization of football.

Spokesmen for the old-boy game, recognizing the growth of commercialism, reacted angrily. The following statements, although written by men prejudiced in favor of a more gentlemanly sporting ethos, underlined the transformations in football generated by the emergence of the sports business:

> On all hands we hear complaints that are in great measure traceable to "gate money." Without the "lucre" there would be no imported players. We should not hear whispers of semi-professionalism but thinly disguised. We should not have a feud of long duration between neighbouring clubs . . . if the "gate" had not been part of the question.[41]

> Football players [have been] invited to make a public exhibition of themselves in order that the directors of the grounds might reap a pecuniary harvest.

It is essential, in the interests of athletics generally, that some strong stand should be made against these gate money exhibitions. They are creeping into all branches of sport, with the inevitable tendency of lowering its character, and giving a sordid aspect to the contests which, if carried on at all, should be for the honour of victory alone without any ulterior thought as to how much the "gate" is worth.[42]

There is no doubt that these big gates are the curse of the game. In London and other places where paying spectators are not so easily procured, football is carried out in a much more legitimate manner, and without any of those monetary considerations which are at the root of all the discreditable transactions which have been reported in connection with the game.[43]

The opponents of commercialization were also opponents of professionalism. The general question of commercialism was debated on the one hand by public school graduates who defended the mid-nineteenth-century game, and on the other hand by men drawn from the business community who had invested money in football teams. By advocating the legalization of professionalism, the latter group sought to protect and expand the commercial structure of football. Professionalism, which to entrepreneurs entailed the competition for players in an open labor market, was the central pillar on which the football business stood.

Individual football entrepreneurs were not guaranteed a profit, however, as discerning spectators could choose among several matches on a Saturday. While allegiances generally belonged to the home team, a club that played poorly often lost matches and customers. Football entrepreneurs sought to market attractive teams to retain the support of fickle and ever multiplying aficionados, a trend observed by a journalist in 1883 who predicted that football had

not yet reached the height of its popularity. So far as Lancashire and Yorkshire are concerned, it is the class of people in receipt of weekly wages who give the game its warmest support, and the feeling amongst them has only just commenced growing. Those clubs which can provide the best and most accomodation for the least money, with the certainty of always seeing a real good match, may depend on "gates" by the side of which receipts from the majority of cricket matches will sink into insignificant sums.[44]

While the potential for ticket sales increased, the "tens of thousands" of supporters who witnessed Association matches each week also were "the first to complain, and loudly, too, of a weak part in any team."[45] A writer for the *Preston Guardian* felt that there "can be no doubt that the people will go where they can see the best game,"[46] and a similar conclusion appeared in *The Athlete*: "the public are bound to flock where they can see the best play."[47] The Blackburn Rovers were made aware of the connection between good play and good gates. The Rovers were without the services of two or three of their former players at the start of the 1884–1885 season, and they were cautioned that if suitable replacements were not found, they would "not only lose a lot of engagements, but they will find a considerable falling off in gate receipts."[48]

A report from Bolton underlined the new popularity of football and illuminated the acute commercial competition among local teams. On the last Saturday in September 1884, there were five "good matches" at Bolton. Despite the number of alternative attractions, over four thousand spectators attended the Wanderers' match, "and if the attendance at the four other matches was only moderate, there were a good few enthusiasts watching the ball in its flight during the afternoon."[49]

The population distribution of Lancashire and the development of transportation facilities that linked several mill towns heightened commercial competition among teams. From Blackburn, for instance, Preston was 9 miles away; Burnley, 12 miles; Accrington, 5 miles; and Darwen, 2 miles. In each of these towns, at least one directorate had assembled a football team and relied upon gate receipts to meet expenses. In addition to an expanded railway network, trams and cabs provided transportation to matches. From time to time, the sporting press printed stories of fans walking several miles to see a good match.

The message to club owners was clear: in order to succeed financially and collect large gates, it was necessary to display good players. Crowds could go to see other teams if hometown matches were not up to par. Hometown loyalties might mitigate the effects of competition from nearby football teams; still, in an age of newly-emerging mass entertainments, spectators, might choose another form of recreation if football did not prove satisfactory.

Just as entrepreneurs acquired more efficient machinery in order to gain a commercial advantage over competitors, football clubs in the 1880s acquired the best players for their squads in order to survive in the marketplace. With gate revenue correlated to the performance of their teams, directors increasingly violated the amateur statutes of the Football Association in order to lure players whose contribution could mean the difference between winning and losing a game, which also meant the difference between financial profit and loss. Some journalists complained of team directors that "the Great God Money" was their "sole guiding star."[50] The entrepreneurs only confirmed this assessment by devising the requisite methods for obtaining superior playing talent.

Rumors of illegal cash payments to players surrounded the directors of the Darwen F.C. in 1879, as their team barely missed winning the Association Cup. Darwen's ability to attract large crowds inspired other Lancashire and Midland directors to emulate their formula for success. "Creeping professionalism" was the topic of numerous articles and editorials in the sporting press, but regardless of the attitude taken toward professionalism, it was a phenomenon whose existence few denied in the early 1880s. A writer in *The Athlete* summed up this feeling when he wrote, "I firmly believe there is no club out of London, at least no club with any pretension to first rank, free from professionalism."[51]

The public-school graduates who comprised football's governing body were agitated by these developments. Graduates were angry at those who had injected "crass materialism" into the game and had nothing but disdain for the new breed of player whose working-class background had not afforded him a public-school education.

When teams of paid, working-class players from Lancashire or the Midlands succeeded on the playing field against schoolboy or old-boy teams (generally from London), supporters of amateur football grew all the more incensed.[52] *Football*, a newspaper published by devotees of the amateur game in London, chided the northerners by maintaining that

> in some districts the summum bonum of life is abbreviated and spelt C-A-S-H, but you, with your culture, refinement (and coin, especially *coin*) penetrate the haunts of ability and allure therefrom that which you know, however much it may waver, is bound to succumb to the "advantages" you freely offer. [Nothing] would be sufficient to describe the atrocities you commit with your vile "gate money webs."[53]

A contributor to the *Midland Athletic Star* predicted that "once the money fever sets in, we may bid good bye to all healthy rivalry for the victor's palm, and football would soon degenerate as much as other sports where mercenary motives have been paramount."[54] His sentiments were echoed in other journals which sought to protect the ethos of the old-boy game.

The issue of professionalism was brought up before the Football Association in 1884 and was also discussed frequently and passionately in the press and in local football associations. Various plans for enforcing the ban against professionalism and for legalizing payment to players were advanced at ten Football Association meetings between January 1884 and July 1885. Participants in these meetings initially framed measures to suppress professionalism after the Preston North End representative, William Sudell, admitted that his team paid its players. Counterproposals to legalize such payments were offered by representatives of Lancashire clubs. Prompted by the urgings of Lancashire Football Association officials and representatives from other districts· where professionalism had taken root, the Football Association eventually withdrew its ban against professional players.

The stated purpose of the rules controlling amateurism often obscured less idealistic objectives, such as class prejudice and self-interest. Despite personality clashes, cabals, and intrigue within the Football Association, the legalization of professionalism was brought about by the growth of commercialism in football.

"Professional" came to be accepted as a euphemism for "working class," and occasionally in the heat of debate an old-boy representative would betray the real prejudices implicit in the wrangling over payment to players. According to Football Association minutes for 23 March 1885, W. H. Jope of Birmingham "considered that it was degrading for respectable men to play with professionals." Jope's remark also belied the argument that the issue only concerned Scottish "imports"; by 1885, gentleman teams from England had been playing their Scottish counterparts for thirteen years without fear of social debasement. Obviously, then, it was not playing against Scotsmen per se that offended the old boys. What unsettled the well-heeled, gentleman players was the new *type* of player from Scotland, Lancashire, the Midlands, or the Northeast. An adherent of amateurism wrote in *The Athlete* that the "employment of the scum of the Scottish villages has tended, in no small degree, to brutalize the game."[55] Another writer stated that he had heard remarked by "some prominent lights in the football world that none but gentlemen should play at the game, as they are the only personages who can afford to lose time and spend money in travelling."[56] C. W. Alcock noted a few years after the controversy over professionalism had been resolved that the

> abnormal development of football among the operative classes in the midland and more northern districts, particularly in Lancashire, was of itself an element of danger which one would have thought would not have escaped the attention of those who directed the Association.[57]

The best players of the day came from mining or manufacturing districts in England, or from Scotland, where the cross-field passing technique was developed. Budding football entrepreneurs turned to these men when they sought to assemble quality teams. However, given the financial circumstances of operatives and miners, owners realized that they could not expect working-class players to remain within the confines of the amateur charter adopted by the Football Association. The need to pay working-class players beyond their expenses was expressed when the Darwen F.C., which suffered lean years athletically and financially in 1883 and 1884, was forced to reduce player wages. An article in *Athletic News* suggested that this would be hard "on the working lads who constitute the team when they are called upon to sacrifice a day's work for the long-journey match."[58] After professionalism was introduced in Birmingham, it became obvious that clubs "managed on the amateur principle are full of danger, for now-a-days the cash is the great end and aim."[59] The *Preston Guardian* merely summarized what most people recognized when it quoted a well known (but unnamed) football official who maintained that

> no working man can be an amateur football player. A working man cannot afford to absent himself from work in order to take part in a game without remuneration, and the acceptance of remuneration makes him a professional.[60]

There were cases of undeclared professionals who had difficulty in maintaining both factory and football employment: most of the Bolton Wanderers spent a week in training during November 1883, "except for two who couldn't get off work."[61] A month later, in Sheffield, many of the firms in the city were in full work owing to the approach of Christmas, and "players of note were unable to aid their clubs."[62] In Nottingham, only eight of the Notts County F.C. players went into training for a match against Bolton, "Chapman, Venables, and Macae being unable to spare the time, or they would join their colleagues."[63] Wolverhampton was forced to open its 1885 season without its captain and various other players who "could not get off."[64] In an interview with a Scottish player, Tom Veitch, a reporter wondered why Scotsmen were so eager to emigrate south. Veitch replied that such players "serve their time to a trade at home, and when they are journeymen, and find trade bad, they come to England, where it is good."[65] Clearly, the availability of nonfootball work was crucial to many of the Scottish players.

Good trade, however, did not always permit much football play, and sports entrepreneurs claimed that a revised body of regulations was needed, which would allow the owners to pay players openly and sufficiently to enable them to play and train unhindered. This was a primary consideration in their debates with old-boy representatives over the question of legalized professionalism.

Officials of the Football Association, particularly at the local level, stiffened in their opposition, and denounced professionalism. At the Football Association meeting of 12 November 1884, W. F. Beardshaw of Sheffield argued that the "legalization of professionalism will tend to lower the game of football."[66] On January 19, 1885, at a special meeting called in London to discuss legalization, advocates of the amateur code asserted that the "introduction of professionalism will be the ruin of the pastime" and that "professionalism in football is an evil, and as such should be repressed."[67] What may be perceived as a bias against working-class players was complicated by a deeply rooted antipathy to the "principle" of professionalism and the issue of "imports" (Scottish players of working-class background) playing for English professional clubs.

The bias against professionalism was closely linked to the graduates' desire to retain a class exclusiveness, not only to their stated defense of the "concept" of amateurism. The decline in the number of public school graduates who played Association football once professionalism was legalized in 1885 supports the notion that class prejudice was a significant factor in the opposition to professionalism. At the same time, rugby, a game as yet unaffected by extensive working-class participation, increased in popularity among the old boys. In the years immediately following legalization, journalists noted how advocates of exclusiveness in sports reacted to the increase in the number of professional, working-class players. One columnist declared that football in London would

> never recover until professionals are employed, not so much to assist a team as to teach the members thereof how to play. . . . The opposition to professionalism savours of a "dog in the manger" policy. Some of the leading lights appear to resent working men not only playing, but playing better than themselves.[68]

The Lincoln City F.C. impressed another writer because, although it had many supporters, there were many in Lincoln who

> hold aloof from this class of recreation yet who subscribe liberally to other sports. I am aware that in many minds professionalism is a great bugbear, and

these should remember that football as played now makes it impossible for a working man to take part in it as an amateur, for not only can he not afford the costly journeys, but his loss of time also has to be taken into account.[69]

The issue of Scottish "imports" might also, at first glance, have appeared to concern feelings of local pride. As the professional clubs recognized the tactical advantages of cross-field passing over dribbling, thereby shifting the emphasis from individual to cooperative techniques, they signed more Scottish players to their own squads. The presence of Scotsmen in clubs previously comprised of home-grown talent upset many local supporters. A fan from Lancashire who had contributed to the purchase of a trophy was incensed because he thought the prize should be awarded to

> Lancashire lads, and they alone. If the richer clubs can afford to pay professionals, let them do so, but when they compete for the [Lancashire Cup], let the true Lancashire lads have equal chance of winning it.[70]

A few months later, after the Bolton Wanderers added more Scottish players to their roster, a writer wondered it the team would "now wear kilts," or whether the club should henceforth be known as the "Caledonians."[71] A writer for *The Athlete* wondered "what honour can there be in a team of Scotchmen carrying the National Cup to any Lancashire village?"[72]

However, much more than mere community pride was at stake when owners "imported" Scotsmen. While considerable resentment against "imports" could be detected, particularly in Lancashire, the same "imports" attracted a good deal more popular enthusiasm, measurable in the huge crowds that turned out to watch the better teams play. Aston Villa, the Blackburn Rovers, and Preston North End averaged crowds of 4,000 to 6,000 for their matches during the years when the issue of professionalism was debated. Other teams attracted crowds that exceeded 15,000 paying spectators for individual matches, as in the case of Darwen (18 March 1882), Bolton (2 February 1884), Nottingham (1 March 1884), and Derby (28 February 1885).[73] These statistics pale beside those of the decade prior to the First World War, yet they point to the popularity and potential of football among paying spectators.

Teams signed "imports" because they were good players who attracted good gates. In their efforts to secure a superior team, the Bolton Wanderers auditioned twenty-one players in 1882, including six Scottish players and a Welshman. A writer suggested that the Bolton committee "may well be excused for trying to reach the top of the tree," and added that how the tryouts "pay financially we shall know at the end of the season."[74] The comments of one journalist reflected the importance of good players to a team's financial success. He observed that the size of crowds increased dramatically in Bolton once the Wanderers hired professionals. He admitted that however much may be said against the system of importing players—a system I am as bitterly opposed to as anyone—there is no doubt of one thing, that it has been the means of popularising the game, and to a very large extent.[75]

Increasingly, owners pursued "imports" and all other players of exceptional athletic skill, as entrepreneurial success rested on filling stadia with paying customers. Entrepreneurs were forced to pay their players, as failure to provide monetary incentives would mean the loss of better football talent to competitors. More owners, dependent upon gates, came to recognize the obstacles created by adherence to an amateur code, and they pressed the Football Association to legalize professionalism.

The tendency toward professionalism in the early 1880s was not confined to larger clubs; smaller organizations also realized the necessity of paying players in order to compete athletically. Whenever "one or two [clubs] tried to be more virtuous," observed a writer, they were "swiftly ruined by their isolation."[76] The experience of the Burnley F.C. illustrates this point. Burnley "has had more strangers than natives in some of their teams this season," and Padihan, which had resisted professionalism, "has at last succumbed to the pernicious habit of paying men to play."[77]

A committee man at Burnley described the circumstances which prompted his board to pay players: "The fact of it is, the public will not go to see inferior players. During the first year we did not pay a single player, and nobody came to see us."[78] In Birmingham, a club official advised that his team had signed a number of professionals, and that if other organizations would not do the same, "their gates would suffer."[79]

The newer converts to professionalism allied with stronger and better financed clubs. By 1884, many prestigious Lancashire and Midland clubs admitted openly before the Association that they had violated the rules of the parent organization. Moreover, team owners stated that those statutes concerning amateurism would have to be changed, and they threatened to form a separate association for professional competition. Meanwhile, the proponents of professionalism were acquiring support in the newspapers, as publishers were aware of their wider circulation. All over the country, noted a writer in *The Athlete,*

> men are paid for playing at football, and so great is the popularity of the game, and so large sums are obtained by clubs in their matches, and so necessary is it that the class of men who are our best players receive some consideration for loss of work and time spent at football, that payment of players is so essential to the present state of affairs, that I do not think it possible to weed out professionals, and bring football back to its old status.[80]

The reaction against the Football Association's punishment of professional clubs was intense in cities whose teams were penalized for admitting that professionals were employed. The *Preston Herald* complained that even if the North End team fielded professionals, "[w]hy should London teams have the right of interference? If the Preston public is satisfied and the executive of the North End is satisfied, what matters it?"[81] The *Herald* asserted that the rules regulating amateurism were discussed among Preston football supporters, and the result was

> one of strong condemnation. [The Football Association's] proposed inter-ference with the players and its meddling with the fixtures has evoked much indignation not only from the clubs, but from the public.[82]

The threatened secession from the Football Association by its most successful clubs; the pressures exerted by the representatives of those clubs, the press, and the public; the prevalence and apparent irreversability of professionalism; and the sheer weariness produced by years of haggling ultimately led to the legalization of professionalism by the Football Association on 20 July 1885.

Football entrepreneurs were thus officially given the freedom to compete with each other for football talent. The Association's amateur code, which restricted the commercial operations of many clubs, had been lifted. However, another immediate problem facing team owners was the peril of the free market in players. An analysis of the relative positions of owners and players helps to explain much of the urgency in the movement among owners to have professionalism legalized. The existence of a free labor market was a factor of considerable magnitude before legalization and immediately thereafter.

Notes

1.   Each Olympiad, for example, had prompted the reopening of a debate over what amateurism is and whether it can or should be retained. The arguments often overflow the sports pages and are brought before a wider public. (See, for instance, C. L. Sulzburger's article, "End of a Tradition," in the *New York Times*, 25 July 1976.)

2.   Weiss, *Sport: A Philosophic Inquiry*, p. 204 and chap. 12, passim. Also Johan Huizinga, *Homo Ludens: A Study of the Play Element in Culture* (Boston: Beacon Press, 1950), chap. 12, passim.

3.   C. W. Alcock, "Association Football," p. 285.

4.   Football Association Minutes, 1863–1880.

5.   Bienefeld, *Working Hours in British Industry*, p. 142.

6.   Denis Molyneux, "The Development of Physical Recreation in the Birmingham District from 1871–1892" (unpublished M.A. thesis, Birmingham: University of Birmingham, 1957), p. 4.

7.   Ibid., p. 7.

8.   Bailey, *Leisure and Class in Victorian England* (Toronto: Routledge & Kegan Paul, 1978), p. 131.

9.   Molyneux, "The Development of Physical Recreation," p. 7.

10.   *The Athlete* (Birmingham), 4 June 1884, p. 358.

11.   Cf. Bailey, *Leisure and Class in Victorian England*, chaps. 4–7, and James Walvin, *Leisure and Society 1830–1950* (London: Longman's, 1978), chaps. 2 and 6.

12. *Birmingham Daily Mail,* 6 Oct. 1880, p. 2.

13. *The Athlete,* 5 Jan. 1885, p. 8.

14. *Midland Athletic Star* (Birmingham), 12 Sept. 1882, p. 5.

15. *Preston Guardian*, 27 Aug. 1884, p. 4.

16. *Midland Athletic Star,* 12 Sept., 1882, p. 5.

17. J. A. H. Catton, *The Real Football,* pp. 43–44.

18. Bailey, *Leisure and Class in Victorian England,* p. 124.

19. John Foster, *Class Struggle and the Industrial Revolution* (London: Weidenfeld and Nicholson, 1974), pp. 187–189 and chaps. 6 and 7, passim.

20. Ibid., p. 223.

21. Bailey, *Leisure and Class in Victorian England,* p. 170.

22. Jevons, "Amusements of the People," p. 500.

23. Walvin, *Leisure and Society 1830–1950,* pp. 86–88.

24. *The Athlete,* 14 March 1887, p. 170.

25. Bailey, *Leisure and Class in Victorian England.* 6, and James Walvin, *The People's Game* (London: Allen Lane, 1974) and *Leisure and Society.*

26. *Football Express* (Derby), 16 Jan., 1909, p. 3.

27. Wray Vamplew, "The Sport of Kings and Commoners: The Commercialisation of British Horse-Racing in the Nineteenth Century" in R. I. Cashman and M. McKernan, *Sport and History* (Queensland: Queensland University Press, 1979), passim.

28. *Birmingham Daily Mail,* 7 May 1880, p. 2.

29. *The Athlete*, 11 Oct. 1886, pp. 653–654.

30. *Midland Athletic Star,* 31 Oct. 1882, p. 3.

31. Bailey, *Leisure and Class in Victorian England,* p. 137.

32. *Sports and Play* (Birmingham), 17 Oct. 1887, p. 822.

33. *Preston Guardian*, 26 Nov. 1884, p. 7.

34. *Football Express* (Derby), 23 Jan. 1909, p. 3.

35. *Athletic News* (Manchester), 22 March 1882, p. 3.

36. Ibid., p. 1.

37. A discussion of the impact of railroads on football appears in Chapter Seven.

38. *Athletic News,* 22 March 1882, p. 3.

39. *Athletic News,* 29 March 1882, p. 4.

40. *Midland Athletic Star,* 28 March 1882, p. 3.

41. *Football* (London), 25 Oct. 1882, p. 8.

42. *Birmingham Daily Mail,* 4 Nov. 1881, p. 2.

43. *Land and Water* (London), 6 Sept. 1884, p. 233.

44. *Athletic News,* 20 Jan. 1885, p. 1.

45. *Preston Herald,* 1 Oct. 1884, p. 6.

46. *Preston Guardian,* 24 Sept. 1884, p. 2.

47. *The Athlete,* 30 Jan. 1884, p. 73.

48. *Athletic News,* 17 Sept. 1884, p. 1.

49. *Athletic News,* 1 Oct. 1884, p. 1.

50. *The Athlete,* 16 Feb. 1885, p. 105.

51. *The Athlete,* 29 Sept. 1884, p. 633.

52. The victory of Blackburn Olympic against Old Etonians in the 1883 Cup championship match signalled the decline of old-boy teams at the highest levels of football play. Professional, working-class teams dominated Cup play thereafter and it was agreed that they constituted the best squads from this point on.

53. *Football* (London), 11 Oct. 1882, p. 10.

54. *Midland Athletic Star,* 8 Nov. 1881, p. 2.

55. *The Athlete*, 29 Sept. 1884, p. 663.

56. *The Athlete,* 30 Jan. 1884, p. 73.

57. Alcock, "Association Football," p. 285.

58. *Athletic News,* 2 Jan. 1884, p. 1.

59. *The Athlete,* 13 Oct. 1884, p. 664.

60. *Preston Guardian*, 6 Feb. 1884, p. 6.

61. *Athletic News,* 7 Nov. 1883, p. 1.

62. *Athletic News,* 26 Dec. 1883, p. 5.

63. *Athletic News,* 2 Jan. 1884, p. 1.

64. *The Athlete,* 21 Sept. 1885, p. 606.

65. *Athletic Journal* (Manchester), 13 March 1888, p. 9.

66. Football Association Minutes, 1884.

67. Football Association Minutes, 1885.

68. *Athletic News,* 23 Dec. 1889, p. 1.

69. *Football Chronicle and Athletic Advertiser* (Grantham), 4 Sept. 1890, p. 4.

70. *Athletic News,* 25 Jan. 1882, p. 7.

71. *Athletic News,* 27 Sept. 1882, p. 1.

72. *The Athlete,* 6 Oct. 1884, p. 650.

73. Attendance figures, drawn from the sporting press, were printed sporadically and are not altogether reliable. Nevertheless, the trend to which they pointed was confirmed consistently in the observations of contemporaries.

74. *Athletic News,* 1 March 1882, p. 1.

75. *Athletic News,* 20 Sept. 1882, p. 6.

76. *Athletic News,* 20 Jan. 1885, p. 1.

77. *Athletic News,* 29 Nov. 1882, p. 5.

78. *Athletic News,* 10 February 1885, p. 3.

79. *The Athlete*, 14 Nov. 1883, p. 899.

80. *The Athlete,* 10 Nov. 1884, p. 728.

81. *Preston Herald,* 23 Jan. 1884, p. 6.

82. *Preston Herald,* 11 Oct. 1884, p. 5.

CHAPTER THREE

Toward a "Sound Business Footing"

From the perspective of club owners, the legal recognition of profession-alism in 1885 seemed necessary. Yet, legalization alone did not guarantee a profitable business climate. "With professionalism," Geoffrey Green wrote, "there came a new trade, and as a trade it required to be placed on a sound business footing."[1] J. J. Bentley, an influential journalist and an official of both the Football Association and the Football League, noted that with legalization, "in a mild manner we then commenced 'business,' " but the formation of the Football League in 1888 was the "means of considerably 'extending the premises' "[2]

The vicissitudes of the free market in players after 1885 and the difficulties of arranging attractive matches created major concerns for team owners. These problems rendered difficult a reasonable estimate of revenue, and their resolution through the establishment of the Football League provided owners with their requisite "sound business footing." The Football League comprised the wealthiest professional teams which competed among themselves for much of the season. In addition to participating in League matches, these teams also played for the Association Cup and in privately arranged engagements. The Football Association retained authority over all teams, amateur and professional, and formulated rules for football which were accepted by all clubs.

Until 1885, the restrictions of Association rules regarding amateurism hindered, or at minimum were seen as having the potential to hinder, the development of football teams as revenue-generating enterprises. Club owners complained that the quality of play—and with it, match attendance—would decline without talented working-class players, who had to be paid for their services.

While team owners perceived the need to pay working-class players, still another decisive factor contributed to their desire to see professionalism sanctioned. The level of illicit player wages disturbed employers of football talent, and the problem of controlling what seemed to be inevitable increases was beginning to nettle club directors. After reporting that the wage paid a professional footballer was £2 for a single match, a writer noted that some clubs in East Lancashire were "anxious to see the professionalism question settled, because it will make dealing with their men a hundred times easier than it is at present case."[3] Speaking at a meeting of the Football Association called to consider the issue of professionalism, William Sudell of the Preston North End directorate argued that professional players had come to dominate the game and that, as team directors could not "get rid of them, it is better to legalize them and have them in their proper position."[4] Shortly before the amateur code was revised, another journalist added that various club committees "know that they will be better able to deal with their paid men than they are at present [and] business would be altogether cheaper" with the legalization of professionalism.[5]

Nevertheless, throughout the lengthy debates at Football Association meetings and in public discussions, little attempt was made to confront the fact that Association rules already enabled teams to reimburse players for expenses and wages lost when they played in a match. Thus, before professionalism was legalized, teams could compensate working-class players for their performance while these players retained their amateur status. The enabling legislation, Football Association Rule 16, was in force prior to the January 1884 meeting at which professionalism was first formally discussed. Rule 16 stated that any member of a club "receiving remuneration or consideration of any sort above his actual expenses and wages actually lost" would be debarred. Charles Crump was correct when he declared at a special general meeting of the Football Association on 28 February 1884, that the "existing rules if enforced were sufficient to repress professionalism."[6]

While the Association statutes permitted working-class participation in the game and simultaneously could have kept wages at a level no higher than those paid to the average workingman, team owners were by no means satisfied. Their dissatisfaction emanated from the conflicting requirements placed upon them: if individual owners came to view the rising spiral of wages as a problem, it was one that was complicated further by competition among themselves as they vied with each other for the paying public which gravitated toward the better teams. The acceptance of Association Rule 16 implied the renunciation of commercial competition; it would be far more difficult for a club director to sign superior players if he were not permitted to offer workingmen incentives that glittered like small fortunes. Furthermore, acceptance of Rule 16 would mean that those organizations which had functioned most successfully in the free market (and which could offer the highest wage) would effectively be penalized, and football's potential as an investment would be nullified.

The owners' decision to function as fellow businessmen in a free market, reflected in the campaign to legalize professionalism and to promote open competition for players, crystallized during 1884 and the first half of 1885. This collective decision also served to sharpen the antagonism between owners and players who performed for a wage. For, if owners chose a free market framework in order to allow themselves the privilege of competition with each other, then they would be obliged to apply free market principles in their negotiations with their employees, too. The application of these free market principles, however, would favor players' monetary demand. This in turn would push wages upward; yet the fear of the high cost of good players was one of the factors that prompted owners to unite in order to seek legalized professionalism! The illicit laissez-faire wages policy between 1880 and 1885 had favored "shamateurs," working-class players who were nominally amateurs but who received wages illegally.

Policies devised by club directors to counteract the players' advantage in a free and open market included limited and not entirely consistent attacks upon aspects of laissez-faire. Owners as a group wanted to restrict the negotiating rights of players, yet they knew that legalized professionalism afirmed an owner's right to function unfettered in the same marketplace. Wages above those typically paid to workingmen were approved, but a wage maximum was also implemented, and owners enacted new policies to limit player-initiated mobility as the specific need for them arose.

The existence of the owners' need for both laissez-faire and restriction helps explain much of the history of professional football in England between 1880 and 1914. Two contradictory forces—the competition among individual owners for customers, and the budding antagonism between owners and players as collective groups—strongly influenced policy decisions of the new football hierarchy. By 1885, many owners perceived that a controlled, legalized professionalism favored their interests and was long overdue. Even so, legalization was but the first step in the owners' larger battle to make football responsive to entrepreneurial interests and business techniques.

Lancashire and Midland clubs, which charged admission to their matches, engaged in keen competition for players. Expert players could ask for and receive wages which were regarded as shockingly high by some. An advertisement in *The Scotsman* in 1882 illustrated the demand for better footballers:

> Football player (good fullback) wanted for a club in Northeast Lancashire, to act as captain. To a really good man, and one who can teach well, liberal wages will be given.[7]

Unlike many enterprises in which skilled craftsmanship had given way to a simplified, mechanized labor process, the unique skills of a good football player put him in a relatively strong position. The director who would not open his purse to a good player risked losing him to another club. Some commentators believed that the players' advantage was the product of restrictions against professionalism that had existed prior to 1885. "A word from [the players] to the Association," a writer suggested, "and the club was ruined."[8] However, such forms of blackmail had hardly been necessary, as even after the legalization of professionalism, players maintained their advantage.

Owners, increasingly aware that good players were good gate attractions, adopted various techniques in order to retain them. In Blackburn, a sub-scription was opened for the team, and one individual promised to donate £100 to the players. The Bolton Wanderers' executive promised each of his players a new suit of clothes if they defeated the Blackburn Rovers in an engagement in November 1883.[9] The most common way for a director to entice players to remain with a team was to offer them cash. However, he often had to recognize that other directors were willing to match or better his offer. A bidding war for football players, which ensued during the 1880s, raised the level of wages. There were reports of players jumping from team to team, awaiting the next bid, perhaps enjoying the dilemma of entrepreneurs who, in other circumstances, had sung the praises of the free market. The sporting press, less amused by the irony of the situation, decried the players' mercenary approach:

> Jones, formerly of Walsall, next of Great Lever, late of Blackburn, and now of Great Lever again, must be a wonderful individual, considering that football is his only calling. In my grandmother's days leather chasers were content to have their shins kicked for nothing, but it would appear that things have changed since then, and a man who can play football a bit is accounted sufficiently important as to command the earnest attention of his fellow creatures. Money is the root of all evil, and I think it is at the root of Jones' football.[10]

Such condemnation expressed the bargaining advantage enjoyed by good footballers, and the newspapers of Lancashire and the Midlands abounded with articles describing how team directors pursued prospective talent. In Birmingham, for instance, Albert and Arthur Brown received substantial bids from the Aston Villa and Birmingham St. George organizations. While sportswriters acknowledged that the Browns had a "perfect right to make the best bargain possible," the brothers were denounced for allegedly breaking a promise to play for St. George a day before a match.[11] The finest players, such as Dennis Hodgetts, were sought with great intensity: "Nearly every club of note swears he is theirs."[12] Teams that engaged in what came to be known as "poaching"—an ironic term referring to the securing of labor in an open market—were often "poached" themselves. The Walsall Swifts lost "the bird they induced a while ago from the [arch-rival Walsall] Town club," the player having "levanted to that mamouth [sic] heterogeneous combination of itinerant players, Lancashire."[13]

Such Lancashire clubs as the Blackburn Rovers, Bolton Wanderers, Great Lever, Burnley, and Preston North End were particularly vigorous in pursuing players in the early 1880s. A journalist warned the North End directorate, after it had signed several players, that such action would diminish the team's accomplishments. The team would be admired "only in the sense which 'lucre' figures, and as a club which gains its victories by playing upon the weakness of penurious mortals."[14] Gentle lecturing often gave way to sarcasm and anger in the sporting press, as with a writer who suggested that "sheds are springing up on some Lancashire grounds, with internal stall fittings where the men are to be chained up" to prevent their being poached.[15] After learning of a player who signed to play in the Cup competition for two rival teams, a journalist urged the clubs to play a match and "arrange to use him as a ball on the occasion.

Kicking is the only kind of argument that would have any effect on an individual of that kind."[16]

Prior to legalization, as team-jumping increased and while owners denounced each other publicly for poaching, the free market provided a wide range of secretly paid salaries. Journalists close to the teams reported various and fluctuating figures; the goal keeper for the Bolton Wanderers was said to have received £1 per match, while a colleague received 30 s. A Sheffield back was rumored to have received £5 a game for his services. A columnist recalled that the Blackburn Rovers offered "Tot" Rostron £35 to play in the Cup competition. Great Lever and two other clubs, mindful of spectator desertion from their grounds to Blackburn's if the Rovers succeeded, offered Rostron £35 *not* to play for Blackburn.[17] Although few players were rewarded as handsomely as Rostron, by 1885, many owners, distraught at the insecurities generated by truly competitive bidding and the rising wage spiral, resolved to improve their situation. Attendance continued to rise during the 1884–1885 season as the game achieved wider popularity, yet owners sought a more stable and advantageous position in relation to their players. As the free market promised no ceiling on player wages, owners collectively took steps to alter the free market.

A series of editorials which appeared in the *Athletic News* illustrated owner intentions with regard to players: they wanted to develop in football the same employer-employee relationships that were the norm outside of sports. William Sudell's assertion that players should be kept "in their proper position" was recalled as owners began to legislate the particulars of open professionalism.

With legalization, players would no longer be able to "arrogate to themselves the mastery and control of the clubs to which they belong"; they would be "impressed with the reality of the fact that they are only servants to those from whom they receive wages."[18] Players accordingly would have to make a "frank and business-like agreement with those who will in future be their masters and not their servants."[19] The *Athletic News* stated that business relationships prior to 1885 had imperiled club finances, and that the determination of owners to legalize professionalism would alter the status of the parties and the overall business climate of football. Referring to professional players, the editor maintained that the

> "mercenaries" were bound to be more exacting in their demands so long as the clubs employing them were acting illegally, and in a manner which rendered concealment absolutely necessary. We heartily welcome the changes. . . . If the old order of things had continued, the prosperity of the game would have been seriously threatened. Extreme competition for the services of certain players was making matters almost unbearable.[20]

Within months, as players tested the new policy, a columnist for *The Athlete* restated this underlying motive for legalization:

> When I advocated the recognition of professionals, it was that they might be kept

under proper control, and that clubs would not be constantly called upon to advance salaries in order to keep their men.[21]

By signing players on a seasonal basis, single match windfalls no longer would accrue to players. Directors hoped to control players for the duration of a season and prevent competitive bidding for footballers after each match, thereby reducing wages. Informal but collective wage fixing among owners lowered wages for the 1886 season by an average of 10 s. per player, according to one estimate.[22] "It is an admitted fact," a columnist wrote, "that with open payment, more than one of our crack clubs is on less expense this season than last."[23]

Even before the start of the season, however, it had become apparent that legalized professionalism by itself was not the final answer to owners' problems. Players were able to reenter a free labor market at the end of the season, and bidding for talent resumed with prelegalization ferocity. Although wages were somewhat reduced, competition for talent made tenuous the agreements among clubs to limit their payments to players.

Two months after legalization, the *Athletic News* complained of the "stealing, 'swopping,' and snatching of players going on at the present time."[24] The following week, the paper reported that cab drivers in Blackburn had not "reaped such a harvest for many a day, there was such a searching and scrambling for players."[25] A newspaper in London in 1888 wrote of the routine way in which players were "filched,"[26] and in Bolton there were discussions of the "kidnapping"[27] and "defections" of players.[28]

Market realities continued to dictate the quest for players. Clubs competed for the patronage of spectators and therefore required superior teams. Because the finest players were in short supply, they could still command relatively high wages. A writer for *The Athlete* counseled that "unless you deal generously with your men, and give them some substantial interest in keeping up the position of the club, no committee will be able to retain the first rank."[29] A player's capacity to function successfully as an independent agent in a free market was illustrated by the case of a prominent Aston Villa player in 1888. "If it is true that outsiders are fishing for him," reasoned one writer, "the Villa ought to give him quite as much as any club in England." This writer also recognized that, while Aston Villa supporters would be sorry to see the player depart, "as a professional player he is bound to study his own interests."[30] *Sports and Play* put the matter bluntly: "for now, the football rover is free to do what he pleases, and demand the price which he thinks his valued services are worth."[31]

Competitive bidding for players presented a dilemma for football directors which was common to more ordinary industries as well. On the one hand, it was to the advantage of directors to unite in their dealings with a common antagonist (labor); and on the other hand, they were engaged in constant competition with each other to obtain players and spectators.

Another persistent problem for owners in their dealings with each other was the unreliability of agreements regarding match schedules. A club would host an opponent, keep the gate revenue, and then decline to visit the opponent's ground, causing the latter loss of anticipated revenue. Such cancellations frequently resulted from unanticipated Cup ties, as it was impossible to predict in October which teams would still be active in Cup competition in March. Less innocently, cancellations occurred at the whim of a club director, and no authority was willing to enforce contracts pertaining to home-and-home games.

William McGregor, who played an important role in rationalizing schedule arrangements, recalled that prior to 1888, clubs were

> continually crying off engagements at the last moment owing to Cup ties, and poor worried secretaries used to have to rush about, wire, and write all over the country in order to get a match. Very often a match would be written off on the Friday. I have known a fixture wired off on the Saturday morning.[32]

Notts County's cancellation of its match against Wednesbury Old Athletic Club, after the Darwen F.C. had earlier the same week "telegraphed off," meant a "very considerable pecuniary loss" to Wednesbury in 1881.[33] Fixture cards, according to a Lancashire reporter, had "become worse than useless" as a result of being "thrown topsy-turvy" by many Cup ties and county matches.[34] A correspondent in Birmingham argued that professional football could survive only when teams began "rigidly adhering to the fixture list." He cited widespread grumbling against the practice of cancellation, and argued that "if the evil is not stopped it will assuredly permanently injure the game."[35]

Even disputes over judgments in a match were sufficient cause for commercial retaliation. A row between the Rovers and Darwen at the Blackburn ground prompted the refusal of the Rover executive to allow a return engagement at Darwen. Darwen consequently refused to honor its Cup engagement at Blackburn the following season until the previous season's non-Cup match was played in Darwen. The gate, as usual, was the real source of the problem, and the issue was settled only when the gate revenue from the Blackburn Cup match was divided between the teams, and the Rovers played at Darwen.[36]

The weakness of football's business structure was emphasized further when Francis Marindin, president of the Football Association, stated that the Association possessed no absolute power over the clubs in the Darwen–Blackburn dispute.[37] Clubs were sometimes able to avoid similar problems by offering visiting teams a flat fee, but the owners recognized the need for more regularized and permanent agreements to insure the consistent flow of revenue, and it became clear to them that they needed an effective authority to resolve commercial disputes.

Poor entrepreneurial techniques contributed to a temporary stagnation in the football business between 1886–1888. Natural rivalries among nearby teams were overextended as directors sometimes scheduled as many as five matches between the same two teams during a single season. By 1886, a journalist believed that for spectators, the appetite for matches was "stimulated in the most wholesale fashion, until it was jaded and suffered from satiety."[38] Another writer conjectured that, as there had been a surfeit of matches, "nothing but a long period of abstention will place public appreciation on the footing it previously enjoyed."[39] The public's desire to see superior teams from outside the home district began growing in the mid-1880s, but this was rendered difficult by Association Cup ties. Owners sought fresh competition to stimulate declining gate revenues, as match attendance leveled off between 1886 and early 1888.

Worsening economic conditions throughout England in 1886 and 1887 exacerbated these problems. The *Athletic News* contained reports of declining gates because of the widespread depression in trade, "and people, however willing and anxious they may be to support the game, can't afford to do so."[40] As the slump approached its nadir, teams in manufacturing districts, "where 'gates' are dependent on the wage-earning classes," were affected directly.[41] In order to draw crowds, admission prices to matches were reduced in some Lancashire towns.

A greater stimulus to attendance was the decision of the wealthier club owners to establish the Football League. The League was created to stimulate gate revenue and to ameliorate the owners' weak position in the labor market, both of which were major problems that directors had previously confronted unsuccessfully. By developing football along rational business lines and reversing extant labor-capital relationships, the Football League was to be a potent force in professional football.

The Football League was founded in early 1888, and League competition began that autumn. Its popularity with spectators was immediate, and initial Football Association suspicions that the League would compete against it were overcome. Many critics denigrated the new organization as a purely commercial venture, a charge that was not denied even by the League's defenders. "Clubs want to pay their way," one supporter declared, and if the public

> flock to see good matches it is much more than they have been encouraged to do in the past. I should like to ask these captious critics of the League system if it is a capital offense to make fixtures with the stern resolve of sticking to them at all hazards, and, if so, do they really think that the old system—or rather want of it, with Cup ties blundering about and smashing up dates—could do any good to the game or clubs? The League is simply an attempt to create a reason—a selfish one, it is true—why clubs should be additionally tied and bound by their own promises.[42]

Advocates of the League never denied the assertion that its "whole basis" was "commercial, pure and unadulterated,"[43] a view shared some years later by the vice-president of the Football Association. N. L. Jackson wrote that the League was a combination of clubs "formed to obtain the largest amount of gate money they can. It is a purely selfish organization."[44] William

McGregor, a director for the Aston Villa F.C., whose circular to other club directors was instrumental in the founding of the League, was candid when he recalled that by the mid-1880s,

> good gates had become imperative. It seemed to me that if we could get twelve of the leading clubs to play each other a regular course of matches, such matches to be regarded as inviolate, we should get the crowd regularly.[45]

After only five months of League play, the *Athletic News* declared that from a "financial point of view, the competition has been a distinct success."[46] Even amateur purists in London recognized the accomplishments of the League and of individual League teams. A writer in *Pastime* concurred that the League "has been a perfect success in its first season," and that its members "have made a good thing out of the gate money." The writer also shed light on the commercial considerations which were basic to the entire undertaking, noting that it was crucial for professional teams to fulfill their engagements assiduously ("the loss of a good match is the loss of so many pounds sterling"). Yet, his remarks concerning the ways in which the League concept stimulated football promotion were even more incisive: the reporting of League matches, he observed, "imparts a factitious interest to the games, and increases the number of spectators."[47]

League matches were highly publicized. In assessing the inaugural League season, commentators in the press agreed that "inclusion in the League means an almost safe exchequer for the season for a club . . . and a very great addition to the interest in its matches."[48] Success of this kind was not fortuitous. An examination of the rules drafted by member clubs for the first season of League competition reveals directorial awareness of commercial factors in football. Statutes which at first glance might have seemed to be purely administrative actually were instrumental in resolving business problems which had plagued club directors for close to a decade. The following rules were useful in solving these problems:

> The clubs forming the League shall support each other, and bind themselves to carry out in the strictest sense the arrangements for matches made between them, and not allow them to be cancelled on account of any cup competition or other matches.

This section guaranteed engagements and made possible a more exact calculation of revenue. Matches were arranged on a home-and-home basis, with each League club playing host to and visiting all other League teams, thereby simplifying the schedule and providing spectators with new attractions for each home match.

> All matches shall be played under the rules of the Football Association, but any bona fide member of a club shall be allowed to play, providing that he has not played for any other club in the League during the same season; if he has so played, permission must be obtained from the League before he can play for any other League club.

While this rule in the constitution of 1888 was not adequate to end the practice of poaching, its appearance demonstrated the League's concern with controlling labor. However, the final resolution of the issue of player mobility was not to come for another two years.

> Each club shall be expected to play its full strength in all matches of the League.
>
> Every club shall take its own gate receipts, but shall pay to the visiting club the sum of £ 12. Averages shall be taken from wins, draws, and losses, and not from the number of goals scored; the four clubs having the lowest average at the end of the season to retire from the League, but shall be eligible for re-election.

These two statutes established a tournament designed to stimulate spectator interest. The competition for the League championship drew extensive press coverage, while the provision for relegating the bottom four teams sustained the interest of their supporters. The excitement predictably reached its peak each April, after seven months of competition. The provision for playing at full strength was a guarantee to spectators that they would view the best talent on a team.

> Any offending club or player shall be dealt with by the League in such a manner that they may think fit.

Recognizing the need for an authority that could impose decisions on sometimes irreconcilable owners, the Football League Executive was established to mediate disputes before they led to disruption in the overall business climate. League officials filled the role that Football Association officers had declined in the Darwen-Blackburn dispute of 1882. The Executive's willingness to act on its mandate was reflected in the penalties which it imposed on offending clubs. On 31 March 1890, the League voted to levy a fine of £50 on clubs breaking their League engagements. Sunderland was fined for having poached a Blackburn player; the Rovers were penalized £25 for attempting to lure a Wolverhampton man; and numerous purported cases of poaching were addressed at League meetings between 1888 and 1891.[49]
The founding of the Football League did not put an end to poaching, as the League's charter was inadequately defined and difficult to enforce in the realm of player-owner relationships. The charter required players to contract with one team per season and this enabled them to negotiate freely with other clubs at season's end.

Bidding wars ensued, as clubs signed players for the next season before current schedules had ended. Some of the players on the Wolverhampton team, for instance, had reached agreements with another club in late February 1889, to the chagrin of rivals who "arrived too late on the Wolverhampton estate, as all the games had been bagged by the Bolton Wanderers."[50] Aston Villa signed its better players for the 1890–1891 season by December 1889, to insure that they remain with the team.[51] The reaction in the sporting press generally mixed surprise with a dose of resentment against workingmen earning several times more than they might in more ordinary occupations. Upon learning that the Sunderland F.C. paid a player at the rate of £5 per match, a writer calculated, "That's a shilling a minute for playing football, and ten bob to spend afterwards! . . . Sunderland people seem mighty fond of chucking their money about."[52]

Writers questioned the feasibility of a free market structure when a laissez-faire policy placed entrepreneurs at a disadvantage. A Birmingham journalist predicted that if "the ruinous competition which is at present going on is not stopped, it means ruination to the game in the long run."[53] Another writer in the same journal confused hard bargaining in a free market with underhanded behavior, presumably because of the players' success:

> So long as it is a matter of pounds, shillings, and pence, a bargain may be fairly made and matters agreed upon; but when you find men running about from pillar to post and putting the exchequer of one against that of another, and telling any amount of lies to back up their pretensions, it becomes a trifle scandalous.[54]

Despairing of poaching and the concomitant wage spiral, one writer lamented, "this is truly the golden harvest for football professionals. When a second-rate forward receives a genuine offer of £4 10s. a week and others even more, we may well ask what we are coming to?" In order to stabilize team personnel and lower wages, he suggested that "the best teams form a trades union and fix a maximum, beyond which no one dare venture without severe penalty."[55] By 1890, owners were discussing the implementation of a system that would make a player the property of a team for as long as he played. The team would determine if and where a player could find employment, and competitive bidding for players would cease.

Rule 18 was added to the Football League constitution in January, 1890. It provided that any club

> guilty of inducing or attempting to induce a bona fide player or players of another League club to join it shall be liable to expulsion. No bona fide player of a League club shall be allowed to join another League club without the written consent of the Secretary of the club with which he was last engaged.

Transfer from one team to another was possible only through the purchase of a player's contract. The player could not approach or be approached by another club without the consent of his current team; a team was entitled to regard a player as exclusively its own. Although players could refuse to transfer, they could not change teams on their own initiative. As a result, players lost their free-market negotiating rights and advantages.

The new policy created a dilemma for members of the football hierarchy who tried to adhere to principles of classical political economy. Club directors who understood good business practice realized the pressing need for a stable labor force, and admittedly the transfer system tended to eliminate player-initiated mobility. The directors were forced to recognize, however, that by implementing the transfer system (and, in 1900, the Maximum Wage Rule) they were influencing forces which, according to the tenets of laissez-faire, were best left untouched.

The new restrictive legislation in football was adopted during a period when laissez-faire attracted criticism from former adherents throughout British society. Free Trade, a corollary policy accepted by entrepreneurs in the early nineteenth century and, after 1852, by "all important groups,"[56] was being reconsidered by 1890. The weakening of the Free Trade position, particularly among influential investors in heavy industry, helped reawaken protectionist arguments that were carried to the general public. Bernard Semmel has described the growth of protectionist sentiment in England, noting that the intensification of the slump after 1880 and the recognition that other nations were competing successfully against British producers in several key industries served to reorient economic philosophy.[57] Football club owners reaffirmed this revised view of economics in their attempts to alter relationships in the labor market.

The solutions devised for the problems of the football business were inspired by arguments that measured interference with "natural" market forces would be in the interests of all parties. In their own debates over the transfer system and the Maximum Wage Rule, club directors adopted terminology that had been applied to questions of broader economic policy. The language reflected problems common to business and football—how to justify a retreat from firm endorsements of laissez-faire, when adherence to that policy no longer furthered the interests of the owners.

The football hierarchy recognized that the implementation of the transfer system violated player rights and freedom of contract. Directors agreed, however, that player mobility should be controlled and that the transfer system was a feasible mechanism. Owners feared that if players were allowed greater freedom, wealthier clubs would buy up talent and create an imbalance among clubs, thereby jeopardizing the stability of the entire League. In defending owner policy, a journalist urged the sacrifice of freedom in order to assure the general prosperity of the game. He felt that it was

> all very well for people to chatter about buying and selling players. As a matter of principle perhaps it may be wrong, but experience in managing football clubs shows the absolute necessity for it, and it will be a bad day for the League, the clubs, and the players when freedom all round is given. Teams must be comparatively level to sustain the interest—if they are not, receipts fall off, and without receipts players cannot be paid wages.[58]

When poaching was rampant prior to the adoption of the transfer system, the *Athletic News* observed that clubs had to be prepared to lose players "when a man has a right to sell his services in the best market."[59] It was with some reluctance that owners transgressed the tenets of classical political economy to initiate and then defend the transfer system. A journalist admitted that the system "may not be ethically what an idealist would desire. But what sport in this land of ours is conducted on perfect lines?"[60]

Nearly twenty years after the implementation of the transfer system, it was described by a Football Association official as a "quite natural growth [of the] need for good players." According to William Pickford, the inability of team owners to insure simultaneously the right of contract for players and a comfortable business milieu for themselves determined the evolution of certain football business practices. While competition for players prevailed in the 1880s, the poaching that such competition inspired was "more than the clubs could stand." Out of "self-protection," directors devised a transfer system which deprived players of latitude in the market place. "The stress of competition," Pickford concluded, "was the real cause of all of this."[61] J. J. Bentley, president of the Football League in 1909, quoted approvingly from a League handbook of 1893 in which team owners were warned that "competition has been the ruin of many a business house, and if allowed to continue will be the ruin of Association football."[62]

The debate among club directors over the Maximum Wage Rule was also conducted in the same language as the discussion over broader economic theory and practice. Approved by the League and the Association in 1900, the rule stated that a £4 weekly wage would be the highest salary allowed to players. This ceiling was intended to prevent younger players from signing on with the wealthier clubs, who were prepared to offer as much a £7 to better footballers. Like the transfer system, the Maximum Wage Rule was designed to enhance competitive balance within the League. "If the desire for unlimited wages were legalised," prophesied a writer in *Cricket and Football Field*, "it would spell ruin in many cases." The fear was that a "mere handful of clubs might be able to keep the wolf from the door, but even these could not be guaranteed prosperity."[63]

Within one year, the more affluent clubs (notably Aston Villa and Newcastle) began to reconsider the statute and to campaign for its repeal. They justified their position by citing classical economic principles, and they emphasized that noninterference in the marketplace carried numerous benefits. Participants in the debate over the repeal of the Maximum Wage Rule were designated by the same labels as were the opponents in the debate over tariff reform. For instance, the Sheffield Wednesday F.C. directors wrote that they were "in favour of Free Trade both for players and clubs." Citing the club's shift in position, an *Athletic News* columnist stated that "under the bye-laws of the League they have Protection, but under the constitution of the Association they ask for Free Trade."[64] More revealing than the inconsistencies in Sheffield's stance, however, is the terminology used to state their position.

There were frequent allusions to the "Free Trade issue" in football, and the term came to evoke the characteristics associated with a laissez-faire policy. Prior to the passage of the Maximum Wage Rule, the *Athletic News* advised that "what must inevitably determine players' wages—all wages in fact—is the law of supply and demand." The editor included a letter from a correspondent to buttress the point: "players' wages will adjust themselves naturally to the state of the market; interference with the state of the market can only result in confusion."[65] G. W. Simmons of the Football Association

Council, argued that the law was an "artificial restriction on freedom of contract." He added that the argument which

> applies to all other walks of life applies to football—that the vendor should obtain for his wares the price that the purchaser is willing to pay. The selling value of an article is the price it will fetch in open market, but the present rule as to the maximum wage supersedes this axiom of political economy.[66]

Club directors identified themselves according to their position on the maximum wage question. "I am a pronounced free trader,"[67] asserted John Cameron of the Newcastle directorate, to underline his opposition to wage restrictions.

Those who favored retention of the Maximum Wage Rule argued that the regulation was necessary for the prosperity of the football business. Actual shifts in economic realities throughout English society away from laissez-faire were used to justify interference with the market in football players. C. E. Sutcliffe maintained that the "fixing of the maximum wage is common in commercial life" and contended that

> one does not altogether like the business or commercial atmosphere that surrounds football, but it is there, and if football has to be governed as a business, a maximum wage becomes a necessity.[68]

As the debate continued for the next four years, and as charges of illegal evasions of the rule plagued wealthier clubs, the Football Association formulated a resolution to end the controversy. The wealthier clubs, recognizing their own need for a financially sound and competitively balanced League, and having been penalized after League and Association investigations, agreed to an amnesty proposal that absolved clubs of past infringements of the rule. The clubs pledged to honor the £4 wage limit in the future.

The amnesty agreement, signed in early 1909 by all Football League clubs, drew an immediate reaction. The Players' Union, created in 1907 by professional footballers, renewed the campaign for laissez-faire when it became clear that payments above £4 would cease. Owners, relieved of an additional £2–£3 weekly payment to some of their employees, simultaneously reaffirmed their antipathy to a free market in labor. The strike crisis of 1909 developed as a result. (The strike crisis will be discussed in Chapter Six.)

Disputes followed owners' acceptance of the amnesty, and these disputes led more directors to adhere to the policy of regulation. John McKenna, a director of the Liverpool F.C. who had "always advocated the sweeping away of these laws of restriction," reported that he had altered his outlook:

> The exorbitant demands of players have caused this change of attitude. When I urged total abolition I believed that a player would act the same as any commercial representative. . . . With players in their present temperament, I do not see how free trade can be allowed.[69]

McKenna expressed the willingness to change policy on the part of entrepreneurs whose interests were now threatened by a free and open market. The theoreticians of classical political economy had never considered "temperament" a factor on which laissez-faire or Free Trade would be predicated. Tangible factors, such as the militancy of the Players' Union, probably were what determined McKenna's attitude and that of his fellow directors. A recognition of self-interest rather than ideological principle led to the rejection of a free market structure in football, as it had in other spheres of economic policy.

N. L. Jackson, vice-president of the Football Associaiton, had for some time urged owners to recognize clearly the business aspects of football. He warned that under any policy regarding wages, the financial interests of club owners had to be considered and respected:

> Let us look at it in a straightforward business manner, and admit straightaway that only self-interest, or self-preservation will persuade the richer clubs to devote a portion of their wealth to keeping their poorer brethren alive. Professional football is a business, pure and simple, and as such I respect it; but when one reads sentimental suggestions under the heading of "Football Fellowship" one wishes to remove the cloak of humbug and show the plain figure to the world, as it may well be shown, for there is no reason to be ashamed of carefully attending to one's business.[70]

In order to achieve and maintain a "sound business footing," it had been necessary for owners to establish a league structure that organized various aspects of football promotion. The Maximum Wage Rule and the transfer system, as enforced by the League, augmented the owners' control of the game.

Notes

1.   Geoffrey Green, *The History of the Football Association* (London: Naldrett Press, 1953), p. 124.

2.   J. J. Bentley, "Is Football a Business?" *World's Work* (September 1912), p. 238.

3.   *Athletic News,* 10 Feb. 1885, p. 1.

4.   Football Association Minutes, 1885.

5.   *Athletic News,* 16 June 1885, p. 1.

6.   Football Association Minutes, 1884.

7.   *The Scotsman* (Edinburgh), 13 Oct. 1882, p. 10.

8.   *Athletic News,* 11 Jan. 1887, p. 1.

9.   Cf. *Athletic News,* 1 March 1882, p. 1, and 7 November 1883, p. 1.

10.   *Athletic News,* 25 Oct. 1882, p. 1.

11.   *The Athlete,* 6 Oct. 1884, p. 649.

12.   *The Athlete,* 31 Jan. 1883, p. 93.

13.   *Midland Athletic Star,* 24 Oct. 1882, p. 3.

14.   *Athletic News,* 12 Sept. 1883, p. 1.

15. *The Athlete*, 24 Oct. 1883, p. 850.

16. *The Athlete*, 29 Aug. 1883, p. 739.

17. *Athletic News*, 17 Sept. 1900, p. 4.

18. *Athletic News*, 7 April 1885, p. 4.

19. *Athletic News*, 14 July 1885, p. 4.

20. *Athletic News*, 28 July 1885, p. 4.

21. *The Athlete*, 28 Dec. 1885, p. 825.

22. *Athletic News*, 16 March 1886, p. 4.

23. *Athletic News*, 29 Sept. 1885, p. 1.

24. *Athletic News*, 1 Sept. 1885, p. 1.

25. *Athletic News*, 8 Sept. 1885, p. 1.

26. *Pastime* (London), 19 Dec. 1888, p. 422.

27. *Football Field and Sports Telegram* (Bolton), 8 Jan. 1887, p. 7.

28. *Cricket and Football Field* (Bolton), 13 Aug. 1887, p. 3.

29. *The Athlete*, 18 Oct., 1886, p. 666.

30. *Sports and Play*, 7 Feb., 1888, p. 87.

31. *Sports and Play*, 1 May, 1888, p. 281.

32. William McGregor, "The League and the League System," in *The Book of Football* (London: Amalgamated Press, 1906), p. 171.

33. *Midland Athletic Star*, 28 Dec., 1881, p. 2.

34. *Cricket and Football Field*, 21 April 1888, p. 2.

35. *Sports and Play* 20 March, 1888, p. 184.

36. *Athletic News*, 18 Jan. 1882, p. 6.

37. Ibid.

38. *Athletic News*, 9 Feb. 1886, p. 4.

39. *Bolton Chronicle*, 13 Aug. 1887, p. 8.

40. *Athletic News*, 28 Sept. 1886, p. 7.

41. *Pastime*, 10 March 1886, p. 140.

42. *Athletic News*, 24 April 1888, p. 1.

43. *Birmingham Daily Mail*, 31 Aug. 1888, p. 2.

44. *Athletic News*, 5 Feb. 1900. p. 1.

45. McGregor, "The League and the League System," p. 171.

46. *Athletic News*, 28 Jan. 1889, p. 4.

47. *Pastime*, 10 April 1889, p. 222.

48. *Sports and Play*, 7 May 1889, p. 218.

49. Football League Minutes, 1888–1891.

50. *Athletic News*, 4 March 1889, p. 1.

51. *Sports and Play*, 17 Dec. 1889, p. 697.

52. *Sports and Play*, 8 Oct. 1889, p. 575.

53. *Sports and Play*, 14 Jan. 1890, p. 746.

54. *Sports and Play*, 21 Jan. 1890, p. 761.

55. *Athletic News*, 7 April, 1890, p. 1.

56. Norman McCord, *Free Trade* (Devon: Newton Abbott, 1970), p. 98.

57. Bernard Semmel, *Imperialism and Social Reform* (Garden City: Doubleday, 1968), passim.

58. *Athletic News*, 6 May 1895, p. 1.

59. *Athletic News*, 15 May 1888, p. 1.

60. *Athletic News*, 12 Nov. 1900, p. 1.

61. *The Football Echo* (Sunderland), 13 March 1909, p. 1.

62. *Cricket and Football Field,* 16 Jan. 1909, p. 1.
63. *Cricket and Football Field,* 20 March 1909, p. 1.
64. *Athletic News,* 23 May 1904, p. 4.
65. *Athletic News,* 22 May 1899, p. 1.
66. *Athletic News,* 24 Oct. 1904, p. 7.
67. *Athletic News,* 15 Jan. 1906, p. 6.
68. *Athletic News,* 24 Oct. 1904, p. 7.
69. *Athletic News,* 2 Jan. 1910, p. 3.
70. *Athletic News,* 25 Sept. 1899, p. 4.

CHAPTER FOUR

Directors

Team directors often asserted that football was sport, not business. They defended this claim by emphasizing that they were not paid salaries and that the bylaws of the Football Association prohibited the payment of dividends on their investments in excess of 5 percent. The time and energy expended by directors on team management were considered ample proof of their dedication and sporting motives. William McGregor, a director of the Aston Villa F.C. and a founder of the Football League, defended this position:

> The dictum of the Association that directors shall not be paid is a wise one. It is wise because it brings into the work the right class of men—that is to say, men who love football for its own sake, and for the pleasing prominence a position on the directorate brings.[1]

A writer for the *Athletic News* repeated the essence of McGregor's statement when he asserted that the capital invested in football clubs was "put there for sport, and not for profit."[2]

However, both McGregor and the *Athletic News* qualified their statements regarding the "sports versus business" issue. McGregor admitted that he was "not saying that here and there you will not find a man who is a director for the money he indirectly makes out of it; but that cannot always be avoided."[3] As a players' strike grew imminent in the summer of 1909, the *Athletic News* urged rejection of Manchester M. P. George Wardle's offer to mediate the dispute because Wardle did not understand the

> exigencies of a game in which there is so much money. Professionalism and sport are not synonymous and if a professionalised game is to live, money must be controlled and players must be servants—not masters.[4]

Team owners and journalists emphasized that the "right class of men" loved football and that these men exhibited an altruistic outlook in their capacity as directors. Yet, the same men also ran their teams as businesses, and it was the commercialization process which would exert an overriding influence on professional football. An analysis of team operations and the relationship between owners and players shows professional football to be a business that dealt in sports much the way other enterprises traded in houses, food, or pencils.

Professional football teams replicated class arrangements which existed in other spheres of life. Directors hired players to compete for their clubs and reminded them that they were "servants" with no say in the conduct of team affairs. The men who dominated club committees generally were drawn from the bourgeoisie, while the men who received wages as players were of working-class backgrounds. The "natural order" of the workplace found its extension in football.

Professional football clubs were operated by committees of directors elected annually from among all shareholders. Committees were responsible for all aspects of a club's existence from the purchase of the grounds to the sale of refreshments at matches. The focus of this chapter is on the occupational backgrounds and football-related activities of the directorates of the major Football League clubs to 1914. Such management committees generally constituted an upper stratum of personal wealth and influence in the football business. Members of the working class invested in League clubs in a few instances, but their investment did not constitute a significant force in team management. Rather, directorates reflected a middle class constituency. (The occupational makeup of team directorates is discussed in detail later in this chapter; see especially Charts 1–3.)

The emergence of the leisure market in the 1880s encouraged the creation or expansion of playground space and the construction of privately sponsored recreational facilities. Those who financed such recreational emporiums as football grounds, amusement parks, and music halls recognized their commercial potential and charged admission fees. When a football team inserted into its memorandum of association notice that one of the purposes of the club was to "fix and enforce a scale of charges for admission" to its grounds,[5] this merely expressed in legal terms what had become common practice. Just as a wage system actualized play-owner relationships, so too did the payment for admission to football grounds create consumers out of spectators. The patronage of the football public was avidly pursued by the management committees of League clubs which competed with each other for the best playing talent and the greatest amount of gate revenue.

Sporting motives notwithstanding, team directors and sportswriters conceded that some money could be made through football. Yet they stressed that by and large, directors had other, nobler motives for participating in the game. The impression they sought to convey was one which emphasized

> the work which many good sporting men do in founding and maintaining our big clubs. . . . I think we owe a lot to those men who plank down the red gold and give so much time to the game, which at best pays them five per cent., and mostly turns their hair grey with trouble.[6]

The sacrifices of club directors were not nearly so noble. The 5 percent limit on profits was circumvented easily by directors whose familiarity with business techniques also gave them knowledge of ways to make and conceal extra income. While profits of football clubs as limited companies were indeed restricted by the Football Association to 5 percent, directors as individuals or as representatives of companies which contracted with their own clubs were under no such restraint. The possibility of accruing "indirect" revenue through one's football ties was always present and often exploited. The potential for using a team as a source of income, particularly during the economically unstable years around the turn of the century, was not entirely lost on the press. One writer wondered

> what is there preventing a gentlemen owning a suitable site in a likely district [from] laying it out and running a club primarily for profit? In these hard times, five per cent is good interest. And in addition to it there may be ground rent and other charges that all help to swell the return of the outlay.[7]

The pursuit of a modest return on football investments with the possibility of further indirect gain renders the claims of sacrifice on the part of team directors and their spokesmen in the press unconvincing. Nevertheless, the frequency and shrillness of such altruistic claims are noteworthy as a defense of the status quo in commercial-professional football. Their implicit plea was for a cessation of criticism and a rejection of player challenges to revamp football. To preserve the football business with the "right class of men" at the controls was to preserve a realm wherein "master" and "servant" knew their places.

Although middle-class control of the football business sometimes was purchased at the price of only a modest short-term gain, investment in teams also could yield social and political benefits of a more lasting nature. Club directors soon became aware that the success of their teams on the field tended to reflect on the committees of shareholders, which were praised lavishly in the sporting press. Such "pleasing prominence" was a unique, distinguishing mark for an entrepreneur whose reputation might otherwise derive from less favorable associations. A civic and philanthropic image of the bourgeoisie was fostered not only by the participation of the middle classes in numerous political institutions or religious, educational, and charity organizations, but after 1880, through the control of football clubs as well. Hence team directors could be lauded as "gentlemen who give their time and money without the slightest hope of remuneration"[8] in their efforts to bring recreation to the masses. This admiring view of the football entrepreneur obscured the fact that once directors invested in teams, they practiced the same business techniques which were applied elsewhere.

By 1880 big-time football was distinctly bourgeois in organization and structure. Both working-class professional players and supporters of the game had accepted wage labor and the admission fee as the norm. The ruling class extended its influence and control into important recreational activities at a time when greater leisure was available to many workers. While trade unions in other industrialized nations such as Germany were becoming the hub of worker activities in sports, the arts, and in some areas of education, it was conceivable that a culture which was essentially resistant to bourgeois influence could develop in England, too. Numerous middle-class reformers were keenly aware of the potentially disruptive effects of independent working-class control of recreation, and for some decades they had provided clubs, libraries, and other recreational activities to the proletariat, with only limited results.[9] Sports entrepreneurs were more successful. The sport that captivated millions of working people also incorporated and institutionalized the principles of social organization that were the bases of bourgeois hegemony. The establishment of such arrangements seems to have been worth a meager 5 percent return.

From information available at Companies House in London, it is possible to draw a social profile of football club directors. Most large professional clubs registered as limited companies by 1914, and names and occupations of club directors were entered with registration. Subsequent changes in club directorates were recorded, with the occupations of the new board members included in the listings. The filing of changes in team directorates did not occur on a regular basis, however, and it is possible that not all the names of new directors appeared in Companies House files.[10] Although the historical record in this instance may be irregular and incomplete, the available files do provide more than sufficient data for generalization about football team boards.

An examination of all existing files of teams that played in the First Division of the Football League between 1888 and 1914 provided the material for Table 1.* In all, twenty-eight team directorates were analyzed.[11] An analysis of directors' occupations is necessarily imprecise because of the occasional use of general categories rather than specific occupational listings in the Companies House files. As several directors listed themselves as "industrialists" or "merchants," the general classification "Industrialist-Merchant" was adopted from the table. The "Alcohol-Tobacco" category includes licensed victuallers (tavern or restaurant keepers), hotel keepers, brewers, tobacco manufacturers, and tobacco merchants.

The "Professional" category comprises directors with a wide range of highly skilled and fairly lucrative occupations. Solicitors (26), physicians-chemists (19), managers (17), accountants (11), salesmen (11), and teachers (9) were the most frequently mentioned professions in this category, which also included architects, surveyors, real-estate brokers, pawnbrokers, stock-brokers, government officials, and journalists.

The "Other" category includes directors whose occupations fit none of the above classifications and who earned their living doing less skilled and less lucrative work than "Professionals." Clerks (19) formed the largest grouping in this category, followed by secretaries (5) and cashiers (5).

*The Football League expanded to two divisions in 1892, and by 1905 comprised forty teams, twenty in each division. It was in the First Division where the greater rewards lay, and teams anxious to secure promotion considered financial and athletic objectives simultaneously. "As showing the advantages of being in the First Division," commented one writer, "we may point out that up to the present time Liverpool have taken more money at the gate than in two seasons [spent in] Division Two." (*Athletic News*, 19 Nov. 1894.)

TABLE 1
Occupations of Club Directors 1888–1914

Industrialist-Merchant	Alcohol-Tobacco	Gentlemen	Professionals	Working-class	Other
175 (38 %)	59 (12.9 %)	16 (3.5 %)	137 (30 %)	27 (5.9 %)	41 (9 %)

It is obvious from Table 1 that entrepreneurs took an extremely active role in the running of football teams. Builders (21), occupied more seats on directorates than individuals involved in any other business in the Industrialist-Merchant category. The alcohol and tobacco trades contributed a sufficient number of football club directors to merit a category of their own.

Not surprisingly, local economic interests were reflected in the occupations of directors in the "Industrialist-Merchant" category. Sunderland had a high proportion of shipbuilders and owners, Notts County of lace and hosiery entrepreneurs, Sheffield Wednesday of cutlery and steel manufacturers, Blackburn of cotton mill owners, and Grimsby Town of men involved in the fishing industry.

Twenty-seven directors can be considered as members of the working class. Of these, many practiced highly skilled trades and represented the upper echelons of the working class. Four were engineers, two were foremen, and there were two job masters, a master painter, a silver plater, and a stone mason. Of the three cotton spinners listed, one was also a justice of the peace, and one tailor was also listed as a councillor.

In a few instances, directors were listed whose working-class occupations were unlikely to have afforded them sufficient capital to participate in team directorates, and it is reasonable to ask from where the funds for their investment might have come. For example, to qualify as a director of the Oldham Athletic F.C., an investor was required to own £10 in team stock. In 1906, the team board included two cotton spinners (neither of whom was the aforementioned justice of the peace) and one joiner. It is hardly likely that these working-class directors had accumulated enough spare capital from their employment alone to undertake such an investment. Yet the company records are silent on the question of whether they might have been installed on the board by the mill owner who was also an Oldham Athletic F.C. director. Nor do the files hint at any other possible source of income which provided funds for this investment. Similarly, on the Arsenal F.C., where £25 was the minimum investment for membership on the board, the records list one engineer as a director. While an engineer was a skilled worker, it is again unlikely that even a highly trained artisan could have provided sufficient funds for an investment of this magnitude.

As investment in football clubs increased during the first decade of the twentieth century, more individuals of substantial wealth registered their clubs in the names of all the directors, while retaining virtually unilateral control themselves. Journalists recognized that wealthy individuals included in their boards of directors other men whom they could influence easily. On occasion, the outlay may have been nominal on the part of all shareholders but one, and it was "in the power of the one to select his co-company floaters, and to hold practically a control over the whole concern."[12]

Careful selections of codirectors by wealthy individuals could insure control over a club. Thus, John Houlding, the principal owner of the Liverpool F.C. and a wealthy brewer, nominated Albert Berry, a solicitor for the Liverpoor Brewers Association, another solicitor named Edwin Berry, and William Houlding, another brewer and presumably a relative, to the Liverpool F.C. board of directors. By installing his own hand-picked board members, Houlding was able to insure a large measure of personal control of the team. As a Liverpool director Houlding never had to meet the type of challenge that he had faced some years before, when he was ousted from the Everton F.C. board.

Another wealthy director, Henry A. Mears, personally financed the Chelsea F.C. when it was formed in 1905. Mears listed his occupation as "building contractor." Thomas Kinton, another member of the original Chelsea directorate, listed his occupation as "contractor's manager." While no company names were included in the files, it may be surmised that Mears was Kinton's employer. The Chelsea board also included Joseph Mears, brother of the principal owner. Perhaps even more noteworthy is the presence of a shipping clerk, M. Kirby, on the list of original Chelsea directors. There is no indication in the files as to how Kirby financed the required purchase of £100 of the stock in order to become a founding member of the Chelsea F.C.

J. H. Davies, the chairman of Manchester Breweries, Ltd., also ran the Manchester United F.C. Other members of the United directorate were James Brown, a manager for the Davies breweries; W. R. Deacon, the managing director of the Davies breweries; James Taylor and Charles Jones, who were also employed at the Davies breweries; J. J. Bentley, a noted sports journalist and president of the Football League who had been hired by Davies to manage day-to-day football affairs for £300 per annum; and G. H. Lawton, an accountant. Of the 160 shares issued by Manchester United, Ltd., Davies owned 100 while the six other members of the board each owned 10 shares of stock.[13]

Apparently, then, affluent men actually controlled the larger teams. In order to increase their power on a club, they placed on their boards men who served them in other capacities. Although "Professionals" were sometimes numerically dominant on a board (as they were on that of Manchester United), managers, accountants, and solicitors could not direct a team without the consent of the team's majority stockholder.

The process of incorporation further strengthened the position of the handful of men who controlled the business. At the time of incorporation, directors determined the number and price of a team's shares. This price generally was out of reach for all but reasonably comfortable investors. For example, on 13 April 1899, Sheffield United stated its nominal capital at £20,000 divided into 467 shares at £20 and 1,046 shares at £10. Aston Villa shares were listed at £5, as were Notts County and Glossop North End shares. Shares in Sheffield Wednesday F.C. sold at £10 and £5.

Perhaps to insure that the "right class of men" would control football teams, some clubs with shares of stock listed at £1 included addenda in their memoranda of association restricting broader participation in club management. To sit on the Chelsea F.C. board of directors, for instance, an individual had to possess at least one hundred shares. Fifty shares were required for a place on the Sunderland directorate, while Bolton and Arsenal placed the minimum number at twenty-five. Board members of the Manchester United, Bradford City, Oldham Athletic, and Tottenham Hotspur clubs each owned ten shares, while five shares represented the minimum investment for the Stoke City, Bristol City, and Bury board members.

Information on the Middlesbrough F.C. was not included in Table 1, although its listings appear in the Companies House files. The ommission is intentional, and serves to illustrate how the financial and athletic development of a team produced basic changes in the composition of its directorate. Middlesbrough, as much as any team that was to join in Football League, initially resisted the trend toward commercialism. In 1889, its directorate split over the issue of amateurism, the wealthier members leaving to form the Ironopolis F. C., a commercial, professional organization. Eventually, the remaining members of the Middlesbrough board bowed to pressures of athletic competition and accepted professionalism in 1892, as the team had been unable to retain its players who were being offered wages by other teams.

Between 1889 and 1892, the Middlesbrough F. C. had an unusually high number of working-class directors. These men were all the more active in club affairs with the departure of wealthier directors who founded Ironopolis. Table 2 shows the makeup of the Middlesbrough board at the time of registration at Companies House in 1892.

TABLE 2
Middlesbrough F. C. Directors, 1892

Industrialist-Merchant	Alcohol-Tobacco	Gentlemen	Professional	Working-class	Other
2 (8.3 %)	0	0	4 (16.6 %)	16 (66.6 %)	2 (8.3 %)

Middlesbrough's success after 1892 led to a radical alteration in the composition of its directorate. Probably by 1899, when Middlesbrough was admitted to the Second Division of the Football League, and certainly by 1902, when the club gained promotion to the First Division, the potential of football had become obvious to men of wealth and status in that city. Unfortunately, there are no Companies House entries between 1893 and

1900, and the evolution of the board cannot be traced for that period. However, Table 3, which indicates the occupations of all directors listed for Middlesbrough between 1901 and 1914, reveals a dramatic shift in the composition of the board.

TABLE 3
Middlesbrough F. C. Directors, 1901–1914

Industrialist-Merchant	Alcohol-Tobacco	Gentlemen	Professional	Working class	Other
12 (33.3 %)	10 (27.7 %)	3 (8.3. %)	7 (19.4 %)	1 (2.7 %)	3 (8.3 %)

No such change over time occurred in the directorates of other boards. In most instances, members of the Industrialist-Merchant and/or Alcohol-Tobacco categories dominated club boards consistently. The example of Middlesbrough is significant because of its uniqueness.

Substantial capital investment in football teams was vital for guaranteeing future income. The expansion of the League and the increased attendance at matches prompted the renovation or complete rebuilding of more than twenty stadia for League teams between 1890 and 1914. Such investment was often made by club directors whose nonfootball income provided the capital for improvements in their teams and grounds. The shift in the occupations of Middlesbrough's directors may indicate the manner in which such a project was financed. The capital needed to build Ayresome park in Middlesbrough in 1903 was supplied by twenty-eight men who purchased the fifty £100 debenture shares before they were offered to the public. One wonders whether the predominantly working-class directorate of the Middlesbrough team of 1892 could have financed such a venture. After noting that the Middlesbrough F.C. of 1903 was averaging gates of approximately £500 per match, a writer observed that there would be "no difficulty in meeting the five per cent interest" on the debenture.[14]

Many team directors were involved in other businesses through which they could arrange contracts with their own teams. Eight directors of League clubs listed their occupations as "outfitteers" and were available to supply uniforms and equipment. The expansion of grounds and facilities provided additional sources of income. For instance, the Everton F.C. stands were erected by Benjamin Kelly, a future member of the Everton board and one of twenty-one builders who sat on team directorates prior to 1914.

The growth of ancillary revenue from football left directors vulnerable to charges of conflict of interest. Management committees wrote statements into their memoranda of association asserting their right to supply their teams through their own outside holdings. Bristol City's reads in part:

> No director shall be disqualified by his office from contracting with the Company either as vendor or purchaser, or otherwise, nor shall any contract or

arrangement entered into by or on behalf of the Company in which any Director shall be in any way interested be avoided, by reason of such Director holding that office, or of the fiduciary relations thereby established.

Sheffield Wednesday's Memorandum of Association contains clauses which expressed the means by which club directors established subsidiary enterprises through their football operations:

The objects for which the Company is established are: (n) To carry on the business of Restaurant Proprietors upon, or in connection with, any premises of the Company, and for that purpose to buy and sell comestibles, cigars, tobacco, wine, spirits, and beverages of all kinds. (o) To carry on the business of Cricket, Football, and Athletic Outfitteers of every description.

The most common source of additional revenue aequired by directors through their football connections was the sale of food and beverages before, during, and after matches. Allusions to refreshment consumption at matches can be found in newspapers in the late 1880s;[15] by the turn of the century, opportunities for providing refreshments to football crowds had grown considerably. For the Cup final in 1901, attended by 111,887 spectators, the following order of refreshments was provided:

2,500 8-pound loaves
1,000 5-pound loaves
1,000 household loaves
12,000 batons
21,000 rolls
120,000 slices of bread and butter
30,000 pats of butter
45,120 portions of best cake
16,000 portions of lunch cake
1,000 sponge cakes
1,000 pieces of shortbread
24,000 scones
1,728 gallons of milk
20,000 French pastries
10,000 bath buns

10,000 plain buns
60 fore ribs of beef
40 whole lambs
300 quarters of whitebait
500 pounds of sole
22,400 pounds of potatoes
200 ducks
400 fowls
200 rumps of beef
250 chines of mutton
150 best ends of mutton
2,000 smoked sausages
120,000 bottles of mineral water
6,000 six-penny pork pies

During the 1880s and 1890s, teams often played on grounds owned by brewers who received income from the rent on their land as well as from the sale of their product at matches. The landlords of the Wolverhampton and Arsenal clubs were brewers who refused to divide revenue from concession sales on an equitable basis with the teams.[16] Later, brewers purchased stock in local football clubs and assumed places on team directorates. When they sold their product to their own teams for consumption at games, they realized income first from the initial sale and then from their share of the profits as team directors.

The large number of team directors from the alcohol and tobacco trades is easy to understand in light of the high potential for sales of their product. Entrepreneurs in these trades who were not members of team boards also took an active business interest in football. A weekly publication in Birmingham, *The Football Pink 'Un,* printed late Saturday scores and the following week's schedule. In issues of the handbill in 1904, advertisers included over four hundred pub, hotel, and restaurant proprietors and over one hundred tobacconists. Clearly, having one's establishment listed in a football publication was good business in Birmingham.

Disputes over control of revenue occasionally created divisions within team directorates. John Houlding, the original benefactor of the Everton F.C., owned a portion of the land on which the club had built its grounds. He also held exclusive rights for the sale of refreshments at Everton's matches and occasionally lent money to the club. Everton's other directors deposed Houlding when he attempted to raise the rent on the club grounds in 1891. After a long and bitter debate, the Everton directors moved their club to a new location and Houlding founded the rival Liverpool F. C., where, as mentioned earlier, his appointment of Albert Berry to the board of directors helped to insure his personal control over the team. The remaining Everton directors were no purer sportsmen with Houlding's departure, and the *Liverpool Review* emphasized that the schism at Everton was

> purely a business one. If not, why all the talk and twaddle about "King Houlding" reaping the incalculable wealth from his hotel, which adjoins the old ground; and why all the talk and twaddle about some other brewer or brewers finding the funds to open the new ground—brewers with houses tied in the immediate vicinity? Judging by the statements, pro and con, there would seem to be more beer than anything else mixed up with the row.[17]

In 1903, brewers on the Manchester City F.C. board contributed to a heated controversy. The *Athletic News* urged the Manchester City directorate to accept a loan from Edward Hulton in order to obtain a more conveniently situated ground. Acceptance, however, would have damaged the interests of those brewers on the board whose concessions were located close to the old ground. The *Athletic News* cautioned the brewers against a "short-sighted policy," although it acknowledged that "if the ground were changed [the brewers] would suffer financially."[18]

Throughout the course of the negotiations, which ended in the purchase of the new ground, the *Athletic News* reminded board members who opposed Hulton that "there is a larger public than the shareholders', and the interests of the whole community must be considered before that of the brewery companies."[19] Not coincidentally, the newspaper whose writers protested against self-interest was owned by the same Edward Hulton who was anxious to gain control of the Manchester City F.C. Hulton also owned the *Sporting Chronicle* and other newspapers which were less oriented toward sports.

Hulton's connections with and influence on the Manchester City F.C. point to another aspect of football business organization: the relationship between the sport and the press whose seeming objective it was to report on it. The sporting press reached a wide audience, as most papers sold for a penny and consisted primarily of match reports, football gossip and opinion. Single page sheets which sold for a half-penny printed match scores and were distributed on Saturday nights. Football newspapers had mixed success: some, such as the *Athletic News,* published in Manchester, and the Bolton *Cricket and Football Field,* lasted for decades. Others lasted for a few years and either went out of existence or were absorbed by other papers. *The Athlete* was incorporated into *Sports and Play,* another Birmingham paper, in 1887. Still others, such as *Football,* published in Wolverhampton, printed only a few issues. In general, the sporting press promoted football as it was structured and by doing so reinforced the hierarchy's position. The relation-ships among team directors, League and Association officials, and news-paper publishers and writers are complex and difficult to reconstruct. Most sports articles were unsigned or written under fantastic pseudonyms. While articles on football generally were little more than match descriptions, editorial and guest columns by officials of the Association and the League were printed regularly. For example, J. J. Bentley served as the editor of the *Athletic News,* as president of the Football League, and as a vice president of the Football Association in addition to managing day-to-day affairs for Manchester United. C. E. Sutcliffe was an official of both the Football League and the Lancashire Football Association and also sat on the Burnley F.C. board of directors. In addition, Sutcliffe wrote a weekly column in the *Athletic News* during the first decade of the twentieth century. John Lewis, a director on the Blackburn Rover board and a Football League official, wrote regularly for the *Football and Sports Special,* a weekly Sheffield newspaper. William McGregor, an official of the Football League and a vice president of the Aston Villa F.C., contributed a weekly column to the Sunderland *Football Echo,* as did William Pickford, an officer of the Football Associa-tion. McGregor's column also appeared in the *Sports Argus,* published weekly in Birmingham.

McGregor, who helped found the Football League in 1888, later recalled the "help we were sure to get from the press" with regard to publicizing the results of League matches. He saw newspaper publicity as "one of the primary factors in maintaining interest in our doings. . . . The publicity has been one of the main factors in the success of the League competition." McGregor hoped that clubs would "never forget the debt they owe to newspapers in this connection."[20] An editor in Birmingham was very much aware of how the press helped to popularize football. He hoped that readers would "pardon the egotism when we say that it is in no small degree owing to our own humble efforts that the game has been brought into the prominence it has."[21] In contrast, N. L. Jackson, writing in *Pastime,* had a far more cynical view of the matter when he referred to the way in which the "tabulation of [League] results imparts a factitious interest to the games, and increases the number of spectators."[22]

Journalists in turn acknowledged their close associations with members of team directorates. "Most of the [Aston] Villa committee are personal friends of mine," admitted a Birmingham correspondent for the *Athletic News.*[23] Whether sportswriters were influenced by personal or business ties, they adopted a uniformly hostile and critical stance toward players during confrontations between labor and management. Their desire to perpetuate extant relationships in the football business was glaringly apparent, as was owner access to and influence upon a sporting press which was becoming more and more a part of working-class life.

The press maintained opposition to player interests during the two most crucial events in the history of the football business up to 1914. It denigrated players during the battle over legalized professionalism in 1884–1885, and again in 1909, it seemed prejudiced against player interests as the threat of a strike loomed. Certain ironies and conflicts of interest existed during the strike crisis. J. J. Bentley's annual salary of £300 for his part-time advisory service to Manchester United was almost £100 above the maximum allowed to players by the Football League. The ceiling on wages was one significant cause of player discontent in 1909, but by this time the *Athletic News*, a paper which Bentley wrote and edited, was opposed to the abolition of the Maximum Wage Rule, maintaining that player salaries already were exorbitant.

In its regular news reporting, an antiplayer bias crystalized in the *Athletic News*, as illustrated in the description of an anticipated meeting of Manchester United players:

> It is generally felt that their action has materially prejudiced the position of the club, and that the players in their loyalty to an old colleague have appeared to be unkind to their club and unappreciative of all the kindness they have received. In all probability the players will decide to resign from the union.[24]

Whether this statement was intended to influence the players, or whether it was prompted by wishful thinking, it was wholly inaccurate. The players did support their colleagues who were being threatened with Football Association disciplinary action. They refused to resign from their union, in spite of advice from this owner-controlled newspaper.

In sporting newspapers outside of Manchester, the players' position was attacked even more strongly. In a lead story, Bolton's *Cricket and Football Field* asserted that readers who had followed the dispute "with an impartial mind" and had

> not allowed their judgment to be warped by the ridiculous charges brought against the powers that be, must be heartily sick of all the clap-trap that has been written on behalf of the Players' Union.[25]

In the *Northern Athlete*, published in Newcastle, readers were advised that militant players had "carried their 'trade unionism' to the verge of fanatacism and imbecility."[26] Similar judgments appeared in the *Liverpool Football Echo*, the *Football and Sports Special* of Sheffield, and the Sunderland *Football Echo*. By giving wide publicity to their viewpoint, representatives of the football hierarchy in the press put forward a conservative, inflammatory, and inaccurate picture of the crisis in professional football. While the Players' Union received support in trade union and Labour party journals, the control of the popular sporting press by club directors and League and Association officials deprived players—and the labor movement as a whole—of a forum for the discussion of alternate methods of organizing professional football and worker recreation in general.

Club directors generally attempted to apply sound marketing principles to team management. The Football League had from its inception examined each team's capacity to draw crowds before granting membership. In choosing teams for the first season, the "commercial instinct of trying to make both ends meet" was respected, "the clubs being selected with the idea of their attractive force" in mind.[27] As the popularity of the game increased, investors from large cities replaced football entrepreneurs from smaller industrial towns. At a meeting for the review of applicants for membership in the Football League seventeen years after its initial organization, the tone "was of big populations and money."[28] Marketing potential and accessibility to population centers were becoming important considerations for investors in football clubs, and the testimony of a former director underlined these concerns when he left his team's board because, in his opinion, no town of less than 250,000 could run a top-flight professional team:

> The anxiety as to a wet Saturday for a home match, the growing cost of taking players about, of training and wages, he said, made his life hardly worth living. "Criticism and that sort of thing never troubled me, but as a business man I consider running a big club in a town of 150,000 is not practicable."[29]

Frederick Rinder, a member of the Aston Villa directorate, had reached similar conclusions four years earlier. There was, according to Rinder, a "natural evolution proceding by which the First Division is gradually being monopolised by clubs situated in towns with great populations." He mentioned the rise of newer clubs that had been heavily funded and were located in or near large population centers, citing Newcastle, Middlesbrough, Liverpool, Manchester City, Manchester United, Birmingham City, Bristol City, and Arsenal as clubs that had "come up through the Second Division, and taken the places of older clubs, which unfortunately for them happened to be located in towns of smaller population."[30]

The expansion of professional football in the South precipitated a scramble for markets. Henry Norris, a builder and chairman of the Arsenal F.C. whose "formidable assurance was based on a powerful personality and substantial wealth,"[31] was responsible for creating market boundaries in London. He succeeded in moving Arsenal from Plumstead to the more populous Highbury district in 1913, against the objections of the Clapham Orient, Tottenham, and Chelsea team directors. These other London clubs, having invested substantial capital in building or modernizing their grounds, objected to Arsenal's encroachment and feared a decline in their gate revenues. The Football League nevertheless approved the Highbury site for Arsenal because "ample opportunity and population" were present in the area.[32]

In football, as in other commercial ventures, wealthier firms dominated smaller competitors. "The League" commented one writer, "may have driven the naturally weak clubs to the wall, but it has caused the strong to survive [and] has raised the level of play."[33] Indeed, the aggressive business policies pursued by club directors pushed aside the weaker clubs, while at the same time bringing about a higher standard of play needed to ensure profitable gate receipts. Although team directors united in their dealings with players, they still competed among themselves for the custom of the paying public.

For example, in the major urban centers of London, Manchester, and Birmingham by 1910, at least two League teams competed, and the smaller industrial towns of Lancashire and the Midlands had since the 1880s fielded their own teams within very close proximity. Spectator loyalties were subject to flux, and Association football itself was but one of several popular entertainments that had emerged during the last quarter of the nineteenth century. Major commercial pressures and pitfalls existed for team directors, so that in 1893, for example, the Bootle F.C. succumbed to competition from two larger and better financed clubs from Liverpool. The emergence of the Liverpool F.C., liberally funded by Houlding, contributed to Bootle's demise. The Liverpool F.C. won both the Lancashire and Liverpool city cups in its first season of play, joining the Everton F.C. as a major attraction in the city. Even as large a city as Liverpool could not support more than two major football teams in the 1890s. The bankruptcies of smaller professional Lancashire clubs such as Blackburn Olympic and Halliwell, and the chronic financial difficulties of the Darwen and Accrington clubs during the late 1880s and early 1890s were due to insufficient backing as well as competition at the gate with larger clubs.

The competition for spectators had nationwide implications: teams were admitted to the Football League in part on their ability to draw crowds, and supporters in relatively small cities occasionally witnessed the elimination of their clubs from the League in favor of wealthier and better situated teams. The experience of the Lincoln City F.C. illustrates this point. In 1908, the Football League determined that the Tottenham Hotspurs of London would be a more attractive draw than the Lincoln club, a decision wholly consistent with the tendency to "concentrate the best professional football in the largest centres."[34] Citing Lincoln City's past loyalty to the League, excellent playing facilities, accessibility, and hard-working supporters, one writer from Lincoln felt that it was despicable that the club should "go under before the encroachments of clubs with their ignoble and sole considerations of the 'big purse.' "[35] The club was replaced nontheless.

The financial imperatives behind the quest for good teams stimulated the search for superior players. Despite the transfer system and the Maximum Wage Rule, team management committees engaged in intensive competition for players who could perform well enough to attract crowds. During the first decade of the twentieth century, wealthier club directors repeatedly violated the rules which they had earlier framed on their own behalf. The Manchester City F.C. found that "abiding by the rules" concerning the maximum wage "means something like extinction," given the prevailing practice of illegal payments engaged in by other clubs.[36] One writer noted that the wealthier clubs "begin to kick over the traces on finding that the limited wages and bonuses prevented them from outbidding less affluent clubs in the market for players."[37] Ironically, at a time when the richer teams were "moving heaven and earth to smash the maximum wage rule," other clubs in the Football League and in slightly smaller professional circuits found it "absolutely necessary to take action to keep them[selves] out of Bankruptcy Court."[38]

Other struggling teams, such as the Liverpool F.C. of 1909, faced the prospect of declining gates as crowds found entertainment elsewhere. "With the present players they cannot expect to draw great crowds," observed one journalist in his assessment of the Liverpool team. "Spectators nowadays will only pay for the best article."[39] These sentiments were frequently echoed in the sporting press as the line between a club's athletic and financial achievements became blurred. In Birmingham, the Aston Villa directors were said to be blessed with a particularly gifted squad for the 1900 season and therefore could look forward to another successful campaign, "both from a playing point of view and also from a financial standpoint."[40] Eight years earlier in Liverpool, the press had reported that "gate considerations" were discussed among football enthusiasts "with as much heat" as were the relative athletic strengths of the local teams.[41]

Revenue derived from ticket sales was a primary source of profit for directors. A minimum of 6 d. was charged for admission at Football League matches, while reserved grandstand seats often cost more than one shilling. By the early 1880s, directors who recognized the importance of gate revenues implemented the practice of raising entrance fees as the demand for tickets rose. Consequently, ticket prices fluctuated from team to team and from game to game, depending on such factors as the nature of the match (Cup, International, League, or "friendly" competitions) and the quality of the opposition. The disparities in charges can be inferred from a comparison of attendance and receipt figures in Table 4.

TABLE 4
Association Cup Matches, February 12, 1914

Opponents	Attendance	Receipts
Aston Villa-West Bromwich Albion	65,000	£ 2,800
Burnley-Bolton	32,000	2,153
Blackburn-Manchester City	41,000	1,649
Sheffield Wednesday-Brighton/Hove	39,000	1,560
Sunderland-Preston North End	34,000	1,205

Even in Cup ties, ticket prices and, therefore, receipts could vary from team to team.

For the most part, large professional clubs attracted huge crowds of spectators who were only too anxious to spend their money for admission and, often enough, for refreshments before, during, and after matches. Table 5 lists the attendance for regular League games during the 1913–1914 season and indicates the popularity of League football.

TABLE 5
Attendance and Profit for First Division League Teams, 1913–1914

Team	Total Attendance	Average Attendance	Profit
Aston Villa	524,000	27,600	£ 6,777
Blackburn Rovers	425,000	22,400	2,309
Bolton Wanderers	508,000	26,700	3,773
Bradford City	358,000	18,800	382
Burnley	458,000	24,100	12,883
Chelsea	755,000	39,700	1,739
Derby County	201,000	10,600	−2,043
Everton	489,000	25,700	3,073
Liverpool	480,000	25,300	8,780
Manchester City	509,000	26,800	4,119
Manchester United	536,000	28,200	unavailable
Middlesbrough	281,000	14,800	3,694
Newcastle United	489,000	25,700	−1,114
Oldham Athletic	268,000	14,100	1,482
Preston North End	294,000	15,500	1,676
Sheffield United	410,000	21,600	3,008
Sheffield Wednesday	429,000	22,600	3,792
Sunderland	439,000	23,100	4,893
Tottenham Hotspurs	518,000	27,300	5,087
West Bromwich Albion	413,000	21,700	4,583

The rather modest profit figures for these teams are somewhat surprising, but it must be remembered that they represent the returns for the teams themselves and not income derived by individual directors. Table 5 cannot reflect the revenue collected by directors in their capacities as brewers, builders, outfiteers, or debenture holders. What appeared as an "expenditure" by the club often provided unrecorded income for board members.

Moreover, figures released to the press by the clubs often were falsified, a fact which was confirmed by no lesser authorities than the Football Association and the Football League. Investigations by those bodies into the finances of various teams led to the censure of Manchester City in 1904, Manchester United in 1910, and Middlesbrough in 1911.[42] Other clubs that escaped the censure of the game's governing authorities presented rather dubious figures for a number of items on their balance sheets. The Chelsea F.C., for instance, listed an expenditure of £189 for the team's uniform in the 1912–1913 season, a most remarkable sum for simple shorts and jerseys. For the following season, during which they had attracted three-quarters of a million spectators to their grounds, Chelsea claimed a meagre profit of only £1,739.

There were, however, very real and credible expenses incurred by large professional football teams. Although the transfer system and the Maximum Wage Rule reduced players' negotiating power, the competition among teams for the services of football players had already driven salaries well above the average received by most workingmen. The payment of a transfer fee for the purchase of a player from another team added to the cost of labor, so that roughly one-quarter to one-half of a team's income was spent on the acquisition of footballers and the payment of wages to players. The *Athletic News* occasionally printed balance sheets of teams after each season, and the relationship between total income and player expenses that emerges from Table 6 is probably representative of First Division Football League teams by the second decade of the twentieth century.[43]

TABLE 6
Balance Sheet for Eight First Division Teams, 1913

Team	Income	Wages and Transfer Fees	Percent of Total Income
Liverpool	£ 16,419	£ 5,106	32
Manchester City	17,045	6,204	36
Tottenham Hotspurs	18,531	5,400	29
Burnley	14,931	9,009	60
Sunderland	23,218	7,350	32
Aston Villa	18,774	7,719	41
Blackburn Rovers	16,113	7,491	46
Chelsea	29,126	12,065	41

On the expense side, it should be noted that teams also paid the transportation, training, and maintenance expenses which could reach a total of several hundred pounds.

Although more sizable sums might have accrued to directors through their auxiliary enterprises, and although additional profits might have been camouflaged, a few hundred pounds on either side of the ledger hardly could bankrupt or sustain a wealthy brewer or builder. Rather, the point is that the men who owned football teams generally were wealthy to begin with, could easily endure a financial setback in their football ventures, but were more apt to pursue the profits which could come their way as club directors.

The overriding impression is that a relatively small number of men, entrepreneurs by background, now effectively controlled what was popularly perceived as a workingman's pastime. In commenting on the power and control exercised by club directors, one writer observed that the principal point in respect to any scheme is the subject of control, and it must be said at once that if any guarantor invests considerable capital in such an undertaking, it is only reasonable that he should have, with the aid of the directorate, a controlling hand during such time as his capital is invested.[44]

The role of the team director was analogous to that of the mine or mill owner. Outside of the football business, team directors often worked in more ordinary entrepreneurial capacities. Their adoption of business techniques was intended to insure the success of their teams as well as their personal control of the football business.

Some directors undoubtedly invested in football teams for the prestige that ownership offered. Many considered themselves "sportsmen," and football a "hobby." Nevertheless, directorial participation in football was in most cases characterized by the implementation of many of the same income-producing methods used outside of sports. The acute competition for local and national prominence required the use of highly developed commercial resources and skills.

As the football business thrived, it was increasingly controlled by the same "class of men" who directed other concerns and institutions in English society. In this respect, football existed as a microcosm of the larger business environment.

Notes

1. McGregor, "The £ s.d. of Football," in *The Book of Football*, p. 60.
2. *Athletic News,* 28 June 1909, p. 1.
3. McGregor, "The £ s.d. of Football," p. 60.
4. *Athletic News,* 26 July, 1909, p. 1.
5. Cf. Aston Villa Football Club file, Memorandum of Association, 1896, in Companies House, London. Unless otherwise noted, all citations from team records are drawn from their Companies House files.
6. *Football Echo*, 24 April 1909, p. 1.
7. *Athletic News,* 27 Dec. 1909, p. 1.
8. *Football and Sports Special* (Sheffield), 28 Aug. 1909, p. 6.
9. Bailey, *Leisure and Class in Victorian England*, Chaps. 2 and 3.
10. The Notts County file includes a directors list for 1890 when the team was made a limited company. Through 1914, no changes in the team directorate were filed. In contrast, between 1897 and 1911, the Blackburn Rovers file contains seven different amendments to the original directors list.
11. The directorates included in this survey are those of Arsenal, Aston Villa, Birmingham City, Blackburn Rovers, Bolton Wanderers, Bradford City, Bristol City, Burnley, Bury, Chelsea, Derby County, Everton, Glossop North End, Grimsby Town, Liverpool, Manchester City, Manchester United, Middlesbrough, Newcastle United, Notts County, Oldham Athletic, Preston North End, Sheffield United, Sheffield Wednesday, Stoke City, Sunderland, Tottenham Hotspur, and West Bromwich Albion. Files for Accrington, Darwen, Leicester Fosse, Notts Forest, and Wolverhampton Wanderers either were unavailable or the teams had not become limited companies before 1914.

12. *Athletic News,* 27 Dec. 1909, p. 1.
13. Football Association Minutes, 1910.
14. *Athletic News,* 23 November, 1903, p. 1.
15. Cf. *Athletic News* for 26 Sept. 1883, and 27 Jan. 1888.
16. Cf. *Athletic News* for 23 Dec. 1889, and 2 Dec. 1893.
17. *Liverpool Review,* 19 March 1892, p. 3.
18. *Athletic News,* 16 Nov. 1903, p. 1.
19. Ibid.
20. McGregor, "The League and the League System," p. 173.
21. *The Athlete,* 22 Aug. 1883, p. 706.
22. *Pastime,* 10 April 1889, p. 222.
23. *Athletic News,* 19 Oct. 1891, p. 4.
24. *Athletic News,* 19 July 1909, p. 1.
25. *Cricket and Football Field,* 10 July 1909, p. 1.
26. *Northern Athlete* (Newcastle), 2 Aug. 1909, p. 2.
27. *Athletic News,* 8 May 1888, p. 1.
28. *Athletic News,* 5 June 1905, p. 1.
29. *Athletic News,* 6 Nov. 1911, p. 1.
30. *Athletic News,* 11 March 1907, p. 4.
31. Bernard Joy, *Forward, Arsenal!* (London: Phoenix, 1952), p. 21.
32. Ibid., pp. 23–24.
33. *Athletic News,* 28 August 1893, p. 1.
34. *Athletic News*, 6 July 1908, p. 4.
35. *Lincolnshire Chronicle and General Advertiser* (Lincoln), 28 April 1908, p. 4.
36. *Football and Sports Special,* 15 May 1909, p. 5.
37. *Cricket and Football Field,* 5 June 1909, p. 1.
38. *Cricket and Football Field,* 16 Jan. 1909, p. 1.
39. *Cricket and Football Field,* 19 June 1909, p. 4.
40. *Sports Argus* (Birmingham), 18 Aug. 1900, p. 4.
41. *Liverpool Review*, 10 Sept. 1882, p. 4.
42. Football Association and Football League Minutes, 1904, 1910, 1911.
43. The returns are from the April to June issues of the *Athletic News,* 1913.
44. *Athletic News,* 16 March 1903, p. 1.

CHAPTER FIVE

Players

Football served as a microcosm of commercial society in yet another, equally important respect. Just as relationships within the football hierarchy resembled those of the business world, so too can the relationship between the hierarchy and its football employees be likened to employer-employee relationships outside of sports. Team directors also owned and managed conventional business concerns and hired footballers drawn primarily from the ranks of industrial workers.

While football players might have considered themselves working men, a less prosaic picture emerged in the contemporary sporting press, as newspaper accounts accentuated the success and good fortune attendant to a football career. Reporters emphasized the details of how a goal was scored in a particular match, and occasionally, the goal scorer himself was credited with a cheerful quip. Whether or not the picture presented in the press of the happy player who sometimes engaged in on-the-field heroics was completely accurate, sports reporting usually ignored any analysis of the player's role in the football business or his status as a workingman in English society.

An analysis of professional football player careers reveals that the impression conveyed in the press generally was inaccurate, as the fame and wealth of most professionals was exaggerated or ephemeral. The rewards which purportedly fell to professionals permitted sportswriters to foment jealousies and resentments between athletes and the predominantly working-class crowds which watched them play. One writer claimed to speak on behalf of the "football public" when he asserted that spectators would "hardly fall over one another in their hurry to take up the cudgels for skilled employees, a large number of whom get £ 4 every week."[1]

The difficulties of compiling data relevant to the social historian are compounded by an emphasis on player "achievement" in the press. Formal player biographies noted a player's height, weight, and which foot he kicked with but rarely indicated his family and occupational background. The details which can be gathered from biographies are sufficient to allow the formulation of some hypotheses, but there is no central, all-inclusive source of data for players, as exists for directors in Companies House files. Much important information appeared inadvertently in newspaper and magazine articles.

Prior occupations and backgrounds of players were not recorded systematically, but club memoranda of association usually contained important clauses which defined director-player relationships. The position of professional players was set forth by the directors of the Manchester City F.C. in a manner that typified the relationship elsewhere: among their powers, directors could "elect such persons as they shall approve to be playing members of the Company upon such terms as they shall think fit." Directors of the Bolton Wanderers F.C. gave themselves "full management and control of the Company" in their memorandum of association. They explicitly reserved the right to "engage and determine the duties and salaries" of players and to "remove such persons at their discretion."

Labor-capital or master-servant polarities were not merely convenient metaphors. Team and League legislation was predicated on the need to control labor and the labor market, as the transfer system and the Maximum Wage Rule demonstrate. As friction and hostility over the issue of wages became more commonplace, even the press interjected a consideration of labor relations in football amid match reports. Newspapers frequently included notices of players "finally" coming to terms with their employers,[2] but the press also reported as football news many instances of unresolved disagreements between players and management committees over contract terms. In 1896, after noting that Aston Villa were "experiencing a little difficulty in arranging terms with J. W. Crabtree," the *Athletic News* reported that the Villa management cautioned him to be "satisfied with a reasonable wage."[3] In 1886, the West Bromwich Albion second team struck for higher wages, and the Small Heath Alliance reserve team of 1888 resigned en masse when its terms were not met.

With the implementation of such restrictive legislation as the Maximum Wage Rule and the transfer system, lockouts became a viable tactic for inducing players to accept the terms offered by club management committees. By 1890, when the Burnley F.C. reserve team attempted to strike for higher wages, power relationships within football had shifted to the advantage of management. The *Cricket and Football Field* advised the Burnley players to accept the team's offer or "go elsewhere."[4] In Birmingham, contracts were withheld from the 1900 Aston Villa squad which captured the League championship. By withholding contracts, management hoped to dissuade players from asking for higher wages or bonuses. During the conflict, one journalist lectured the Villa players that they "get good pay and treatment, and they could not do better in either way elsewhere."[5]

A professional football player negotiated with his employer like any other worker. Yet, while he sold his labor to a team, his job did not consist of operating a machine owned by his employer, as it might have in another line of work. In a sense, the footballer was both the operator and the "machine," and his labor was somewhat different from that of other workers. Still, the player/"machine" was dependent on his employer and was vulnerable to the forces of the marketplace.

Exceptionally gifted athletes occasionally were obliged to transmute their talents in order to meet market requirements that were determined by nonathlete directors. Blackburn Rover committee member John Lewis replied to a director from another club who had asked whether "we [have] any power to compel [a player who had balked at switching positions] to do as we wish and if so what is the correct procedure?" Lewis answered that the committee of a team has "the right to appoint their men to the position they think best." Furthermore, the player had

> no right to refuse the instruction of his committee to play in a certain position. If he did refuse, the committee would be quite justified in "dealing with" the player for insubordination, and inflicting a sentence of suspension.[6]

This exchange points to what was termed the "master-servant" relationship in professional football. The terminology, borrowed from the broader economic and legal lexicon of the day,[7] affirmed the difference in status between players and directors. "Master" and "servant" became part of everyday sportswriting jargon, as when Walter Bennett, a player for Sheffield United, was routinely described as a "good servant to the club."[8]

"Master" and "servant" were also frequently juxtaposed in describing the control of the football business. For instance, when professional players insisted on wearing trade union badges on their jerseys, contrary to a ruling by the Football League, C. E. Sutcliffe, an official of the Football League, ventured that the players' actions were tantamount to the "re-opening of the old struggle, 'Who Shall Be Master?' " Sutcliffe posed the question rhetorically; he felt that players should be brought "to their senses" and that "the clubs are determined to be masters."[9] James Grant, treasurer of the Liverpool Football Association, declared that a professional player must not

> forget his position as a servant of his club, and to adopt the attitude of the Union of late is simply folly run mad. They are not and cannot be masters. There is no abasement in the term servant—we are all servants and must recognise some head in our business and in our pleasure.[10]

Directors reasserted the view that they were entitled to complete governance of football whenever players questioned existing power relationships. Noting that the West Bromwich Albion squad contained numerous "dissatisfied players," one sportswriter argued that "men who are paid for their services have no right on their club's executive."[11] During the strike crisis of 1909, a journalist in Sheffield echoed these sentiments: professional players were "paid to play and leave the rest to the clubs."[12]

The professional football player was perceived as a replaceable part in the machinery of entertainment production. Because he controlled neither his own labor nor the business that depended on it, he negotiated the best terms possible for the sale of his abilities. In this context he was a "servant" who frequently attained an identity only as a "position" on a football pitch. Remarking that the Association game is "not to be regarded simply as a pastime as it was a few years ago" but was "unquestionably now more of the nature of a business," a Birmingham writer in 1890 assayed the halfbacks on the Aston Villa squad:

> Cowan must be supported by more powerful players than is the case at present. Personally, of course, I have nothing to say against the men who are all the best of fellows, but we are now speaking of football as it is now, and personal considerations must be sent to the wall.[13]

In referring to the improved play of Notts County F.C., another writer predicted that further changes would still be necessary:

> The weak places are to be made strong, and ere the next campaign opens, we shall probably have a fine fresh fullback, a capital halfback, and a forward or two on the spot as reserves.[14]

Some descriptions of players were even less complimentary, although probably inadvertently so. A procurer of football talent for professional clubs advertised a player by announcing, "There's a young giant for you. . . . This is a colt worth training, and I will place him only in a good school."[15] In commenting on the purchase of a player for £1,000, the *Athletic News* asserted in 1905 that "football players will eventually rival thoroughbred racehorses in the market."[16] With only a bit less imagination, a writer noted that the Burnley F.C. were

> following in the footsteps of several other Lancashire clubs. They are going for importation and confiscation, their last imported article being Ronaldson, and their last act of confiscation was the taking over of Friel of Accrington.[17]

No doubt aware of the process through which players lost their identity, a correspondent in *Cricket and Football Field* decried the fact that players were

> much like a sack of potatoes in the wholesale market—open to be acquired by the man with the best offer [of a transfer fee to his present team]. . . . He does little more than look on while his masters transfer him to the highest bidder if they decide—very often because of a lean purse—to dispense with his services, and make a profit out of him.[18]

Despite the marketing terminology surrounding them, players were more than positions on a pitch, potatoes in a sack, colts, or imported articles. A discussion of their social origins and aspects of their playing careers goes beyond their abilities as goal scorers or defenders.

There is no reason to contradict what had become axiomatic in football circles: "If you want a footballer, just go to the top of a mine shaft and whistle." There are no specific listings that would permit a detailed breakdown of player backgrounds, but most available evidence strongly suggests that professional footballers were drawn from the working class.

In 1900, a writer in a football annual noted that professionalism would be rampant south of the Thames "were it not for the fact that big manufacturing centres are not so numerous . . . for Association [football] is certainly the game of the masses."[19] In 1891, another author drew an even tighter connection between the working class and professional football players when he argued that the introduction of professionalism in London would

> act as a great stimulus to the many hundreds of players who may be said to belong to the working classes. There is now an inducement for these to "combine business with pleasure," to study how to play the game thoroughly, and thus to be enabled to, for several years at least, make a living out of it.[20]

While it seems clear that players on the better professional clubs were drawn from the working class, it is more difficult to identify the particular stratum within that class from which they emanated. As occupational backgrounds of players were tertiary considerations for journalists, such information usually was omitted from coverage of football. It appears that both skilled and unskilled workers attained football employment, provided they possessed the requisite skills on the field. The first professionals from Scotland and Wales seem to have been skilled artisans prior to their football careers; James Love had been a stonemason and Hugh McIntyre an upholsterer. Both played with Lancashire clubs in the late 1870s and early 1880s, as did Powell, who became a "leading hand" at a large brass works in Bolton, and Hay, who worked at a forge in the same town.[21]

It would be shortsighted to overemphasize the precise status of players' prefootball employment, not only because there is insufficient information relating to this question, but also because such a concern tends to obscure a more fundamental reality: skilled or unskilled, working people were dependent upon a wage, even in such relatively highly paid professions as football. Thus, the particular type and level of industrial training of the unnamed Darwen F.C. player who, in 1882, was prevented from helping his team "owing to the disinclination of an employer" to grant him "a few hours leave of absence"[22] was not especially relevant and went unmentioned in the *Athletic News* article which reported the event. Whether he was an engineer or an operative, he confronted the same restrictions from his employer.

Yet the columns of *Athletic News* provide partial insights into the careers of some professional players prior to their football engagement. In an incomplete but presumably representative series of interviews with team captains between December 1901, and February 1902, players recounted their former occupations. As a youth growing up in Manchester, Tom Booth of Everton had been a hatter. Grimsby Town's George Mountain had been apprenticed as an engineer after leaving school, while Ernest Needham (Sheffield United) and William Beats (Wolverhampton) had been colliers.

Aston Villa halfback Sampson Whittaker also had been a collier before becoming a professional football player, as had Preston North End's George Baker ("Like many another good footballer, Baker is a collier, and during his first season at Chesterfield he worked down in the pit five days in the week").[23] The most widely celebrated football player prior to the First World

War, Billy Meredith, continued to work in the Welsh coalfields for three months after he became a professional player in 1894. However, this seems to be an exception, and, by the 1890s most professional footballers did not hold a job other than their positions on a team. Hard manual labor in factories jeopardized athletic prowess; the football career of J. Devlin, who played for Bolton in the 1880s, was shortened while he was working as an engineer when an industrial accident cost him the sight of one eye. T. Cooper, a fullback for the Bury F.C., was employed at the Chesham Hatworks, where he was fatally injured when he slipped into a vat of boiling dye.

Apart from the physical hazards of the workplace which threatened the careers of players, ordinary employment interfered with team practice and even left in doubt player availability for matches. The Accrington F. C., for example, was aware of the problem of having its players employed off the field. It became difficult to assemble the men for practice, as "every one of the professionals is industrially employed during the week."[24] Player dependence on nonfootball work was turned to advantage by the Sunderland F.C. A director explained the success of his team in recruiting players by declaring that Sunderland was not always able to outbid other clubs, but "we find our men employment and teach them trades."[25]

With legalized professionalism, the establishment of the Football League, and the subsequent increase in match attendance, directors encouraged their players to concentrate solely on football. Gradually, professionals left the mines and factories and worked full time at the game. This tendency, which was supported and financed by clubs that attempted to gain thereby a competitive advantage over rival teams, also completed the process of professionalization among England's better players.

The apparent irony of employing men in an occupation that had once been considered "play" was not always accepted gracefully. Although the spread of professionalism ultimately was a consequence of the growth of the leisure business and was encouraged through a more general development of market relationships, the paradox wherein play became work was used by sportswriters to demean the worker. Surely, some reasoned, if footballers were paid to play, their gains were ill-deserved. One columnist maintained that people "object to being mulcted in a shilling, or maybe two shillings, for an hour and a half's enjoyment, when they know that the money will be paid to men who loaf about the week through."[26] When a Midlands player was induced to leave for a Lancashire team in 1883, a Birmingham journalist claimed that the player's inclination for the "easy life" determined his move. He would, the writer predicted, be able to spend his nonplaying hours "sticking up skittles in an alley."[27] In 1899, a club director told a reporter that players "are attacked by fits of 'wanting-to-do-nothingness.' " The director maintained that the "only things [professionals] care about is drawing their wages."[28] During the strike crisis of 1909, Rev. J. T. Hales, vice-president of the Southern League, argued that many professional footballers spent their time in a "most unsatisfactory manner" when not playing. "They had a lot of time on their hands," claimed Hales, "and the result was that a good deal of that time was spent in gambling, and, in some instances, drinking."[29]

The wages paid to players were another sore point with directors and sportswriters. After 1900, most professionals in the Football League were paid close to £4 a week throughout the year, the maximum salary permitted, but one much higher than paid to other workingmen. A. L. Bowley, in *Wages and Incomes in the United Kingdom Since 1860*, marked 46 s. as the cut off point for the highest decile for weekly earnings among workingmen in industry in 1906.[30]. Bowley included a wide fluctuation in wages below this point and cited considerable variance within and among trades. Clearly, footballers were paid at a rate that in some instances was several times that of other workingmen.

Although football wages were high and football labor may indeed be seen as unique, other factors connected footballers to the working class as a whole. Professional players and other workers functioned within a wage relationship, and their wages represented only a fraction of the income which they produced for their employers. Moreover, footballers had little control over work schedules, conditions, or strategies and they would ultimately accept the protection afforded by trade union organization.

Most importantly, the brevity of a football career as well as the damage done to players through injuries created special problems for profesional football players. Players did not see themselves as part of the football hierarchy, which indeed they were not. They did perceive themselves as highly skilled, and for a time highly paid, workers who would one day return to more mundane occupations if they remained healthy enough to do so. Alex Raisbeck, captain of the Liverpool F.C., speculated on his future when he declared, "I have been a collier, and maybe I shall be again."[31]

The working-class backgrounds of professional footballers often invited denigration. Noting the decline of amateur football in former strongholds where professionalism has been resisted, one writer maintained that the "leading lights" of the amateur game appeared to "resent working men not only playing, but playing better than themselves."[32] The Football Association, reflecting the widely held view that professionals were from working-class backgrounds, assigned them blue jerseys for a "Gentlemen versus Players" match in 1886. The *Athletic News* remarked that the Association's selection was a deliberate affront, as dark jerseys

> savour more of the collier than anything else, and the gentlemen were clad in white shirts. The difference was most marked, as doubtless it was intended to be.[33]

The image of the professional footballer that emerged from comments of team directors, amateur purists, and sportswriters—and, therefore, the image that was frequently drawn before the public—was of a man who enjoyed considerable wealth and leisure time. Professional players were also described as lazy, prone to vice, and vaguely inferior to the "better sort" who often maligned them.

The purpose of this discussion is to come to an understanding of professional football careers, in a manner that goes beyond superficial impressions and simplistic stereotypes. Primary factors to consider in assessing careers were their short duration and their tenuous nature. Table 1 shows personnel turnover on a yearly basis and lists the number of starting players dropped annually by three financially stable and athletically successful teams. Important factors that contributed to the rate of personnel turnover were injuries, transfers, demotions, and retirements. Prior to 1914, Aston Villa, Everton, and Sunderland were among the few clubs that

TABLE 1
Number of Starting Players Replaced*

Season	Aston Villa	Everton	Sunderland
1888–1889	5	7	—
1889–1890	4	4	—
1890–1891	3	6	3
1891–1892	5	6	4
1892–1893	6	5	1
1893–1894	4	3	5
1894–1895	4	3	4
1895–1896	4	3	4
1896–1897	2	4	7
1897–1898	—	7	—
1898–1899	—	5	—
1899–1900	1	6	5
1900–1901	7	3	3
1901–1902	6	4	2
1902–1903	5	4	3
1903–1904	5	3	5
1904–1905	3	0	3
1905–1906	5	2	6
1906–1907	5	2	9
1907–1908	7	5	7
1908–1909	5	1	3
1909–1910	2	4	2
1910–1911	6	6	3
1911–1912	7	5	7
1912–1913	6	5	5

*The starting teams were reconstructed by listing the lineups printed in the sporting press. Lineups were derived by averaging the number of games that a player started through the first five weeks of a season. For instance, if "Jones' was listed as the starting goalkeeper in the first, third, fourth, and fifth games, he was listed as the team's regular at that position. Entries proved inconsistent for Aston Villa and Sunderland for 1897 and 1898 and therefore were omitted from the chart. Sunderland entered the League in the 1890–1891 season, and the analysis of their lineup begins then.

managed to avoid relegation to the Second Division. In this respect, they functioned with a greater degree of success and continuity than did most other teams. Player tenure probably was longer at these three clubs than it was elsewhere during the years measured in the chart.

The frequency of injuries to professional footballers necessitated an expansion in the number of men retained by teams. While the eleven starting players and a few reserves constituted the squads of the early 1880s, wealthier teams sometimes employed as many as twenty-five players by the turn of the century.* The increase in the number of jobs available was more than offset by the risk of injury which shortened many a playing career. *Cricket and Football Field* computed the starting lineups for teams in both Football League divisions, for the Southern League, and for the Scottish League during the 1913–1914 season, and the findings emphasized the fact that injuries considerably reduced the personnel of these teams. By New Year's 1914, only 169 of the 1,701 players had "survived the risk of accident or illness" and were able to start each match. By mid-April, the number had fallen to 61.[34] The same journal had observed the effects of injuries to players on the Bolton Wanderers F.C. some years earlier. In 1909, the "greatest anxiety" which the Wanderers experienced was

> not so much as to whether the team is capable of defying defeat in the remaining League matches, as whether they will be fortunate enough to keep their players free from accident . . . the Wanderers seem quite unable to keep the same eleven for two consecutive matches.[35]

The exceptionally high rate of player injuries stirred numerous responses. Insurance companies, such as the Boiler Insurance and Steam Power Company, Ltd., of Manchester, issued policies for injuries by the late 1880s,[36] and surgeons who could treat players advertised their services. One specialist in bone setting stated that "the number of players who are kept out of their teams every week, through injuries, is really astonishing. Many clubs are never able to play their really best team owing to players being incapacitated."[37]

Even the best players were fearful of being replaced and losing their livelihood, and this fear often prompted them to play when injured. They responded to injuries by ignoring them whenever possible. A sportswriter in 1890 believed that a player named Higgins actually was unfit to play, "his limbs being one mass of bruises and bandages," yet Higgins managed to score four goals during one match.[38] But club management perceived the injury problem differently. John Lewis, a director of the Blackburn Rovers, felt that players pampered themselves, and he complained that

> we have nowadays so many stoppages [of play] for "injuries" to players which in the earlier days of the game would hardly have been noticed. I do not wish to

---

*When the Football League expanded to a two division, forty team format in 1905, member clubs were employing over one thousand footballers.

appear callous or brutal, but there have been constant complaints this season of the frequency and length of stoppages, and something seems necessary to be done to remind players that football is a game in which knocks must be expected and taken almost as a matter of course.[39]

Poor medical and training facilities extended the amount of time that players lost due to injuries. Peter Morris has described the rather primitive treatment given injured players during the first decades of League competition,[40] and a Manchester City player's death might have been prevented had there been better care given to an injury: D. Jones died of blood poisoning contracted through a cut he received during a match. Extreme but not isolated incidents of serious injuries belied the notion that football was safe, easy work. The sporting press often carried reports of players who were unable to perform as a result of broken bones or injuries to tendons and ligaments. Notably, the risk and frequency of injury to players represented another aspect of the similarities in conditions between industry and the football business.

Transfer to other clubs also affected a player's tenure. For management committees, the transfer was but one means of strengthening the team, and acquisition of new players and the sale of older ones became a common management strategy. Official League records of such transactions proved unavailable, but postseason reports indicated extensive shifts in personnel. In the 9 May 1904 issue of the *Athletic News*, close to a hundred transfer notices were printed, and scores of transfers were listed in the *Cricket and Football Field* of 7 May 1914. In 1909, *Football and Sports Special* indicated that over fifty players were sold out of the First Division at season's end, while close to one hundred professionals were obtained by First Division teams from smaller combinations.[41] The frequency of transfers prompted criticism of "wholesale moves" which attenuated spectator loyalties to individual players and teams.[42]

All players, even those who managed to avoid injury or transfer, were vulnerable to advancing age. Few retained sufficient skill to perform competitively in the First Division once they reached their mid-thirties. Players were routinely dismissed or transferred when their skills diminished, and their departure, if noted at all, was reported in an off-hand manner. "The Blackburn Rovers are becoming economists," one writer observed. "They have decided to decrease their wage list by giving to the old warhorse Joe Lofthouse and Gillespie their notices."[43] A journalist in Newcastle found it "surprising" when he noted the number of players removed from First Division football who, five years earlier, were looked upon as "indispensables."[44] The *Athletic News* also reported that Football League teams occasionally dismissed players summarily after having obtained them through transfer, "if they do not turn out quite up to expectations."[45]

These factors often rendered meaningless the much-publicized rewards of club-sponsored benefit matches, which could guarantee professionals a few hundred pounds. Players with five years of continuous service to a team were eligible for benefit matches, and this disqualified players who were transferred before that period was up. Although the Football Association drafted legislation which partially offset monetary loss through transfer, Wray Vamplew has concluded that benefit matches fell primarily to players at the very top of their profession.[46]

As a rule, players were offered contracts when committees believed that they could strengthen a club. When their abilities diminished, or when a team discovered a more efficient man, a player was discharged. A player's career depended on the availability of work and on his capacity to meet the demands of the job.

Vulnerability to dismissal reflected another parallel between professional football careers and those of other workers. Yet members of the public, seeking an escape from poverty, had a different perception of professional football careers. The prevalent view that players were wealthy and secure says more about the yearnings of would-be players than it accurately reveals about the reality of player prospects. A writer noted that some men forsake their ordinary jobs to seek employment as footballers, a predictable enough occurrence for those who were

> harassed by monotonous jobs, mediocre wages, maddening superiors, spells out of work; in such cases it seems hard to blame a strong lad for preferring a few golden sovereigns and risking what the future will bring.[47]

Football Players Magazine, the monthly publication of the Players' Union, discussed the transition from working at an obscure job to practicing a highly visible, celebrated profession. An article addressed the question of professional players "being taken from their work, suddenly put into a state of affluence and semi-idleness, and at the end of their [football] career being outside trade."[48] The article acknowledged the working-class backgrounds of professional players and predicted more ordinary employment for them when their football days were over. Workers who held jobs for many years could acquire a competence and security at their work, but professional footballers were less equipped to cope with the vicissitudes of working outside sports when they were dismissed. They had left the job market when they were young and had spent their prime working years playing football. When they returned to the world of nonfootball employment, they had to compete against younger and better trained workers.

A handful of former footballers were fortunate enough not to have to return to the mines or factories. "The luckiest and longest-headed," observed one writer who was not inclined to sympathize with players,

> manage to get themselves set up in public houses, and so long as they limit themselves to selling the drink they do well; but, of course, they form a very small proportion of the whole number.[49]

This writer's remark is indicative of the prevalent view that a successful post-football career was to be found in the operation of a pub. However, evidence on this point is impressionistic, and it seems that most former footballers were obliged to settle for less rewarding careers once they retired from the field.

The *Railway Review*, the journal of the railwaymens union, also was mindful of the brevity of football employment and noted both the working-class origins and post-professional career destinations of many professionals. Most players were "Trade Unionists before taking up football for a living, and they have not allowed their tickets to lapse, anticipating a return to their apprenticed trade in the ordinary course of events."[50] However, players such as Samuel Frost, whose recurring knee ailments rendered him expendable by the Millwall F.C., often were forced to recognize how ill-prepared they were for work other than football. Frost "knew no trade or industry, having been a footballer all his life, so that he was an unskilled labourer in an already overstocked skilled market."[51] Thomas Holland of the Millwall F.C. was also plagued by an injury to his knee and at the beginning of the 1913–1914 season he "was 'retired' because he was thought to be inefficient." Holland had little alternative but to take up work as a cotton operative at 25 s. per week when his playing career ended.[52] One writer stated that "instances are readily given" of professionals "finding it impossible to settle down to a life of steady work after six years of professional play," and he urged young players to obtain written permission from their clubs to continue at ordinary work while they were engaged as footballers.[53]

Players who did seek regular employment in addition to their football work often found "obstacles . . . put in their way" by directors who were concerned that outside jobs could affect attendance at practice and training sessions.[54] A writer for *Football Players Magazine,* recognizing that many players had no previous industrial training, recommended that it would be "desirable for all players to follow ordinary employment during the week," to insure that they could acquire other skills. He noted, however, that a player could follow such a course of employment "only in exceptional cases." Association football had "risen to a height of importance which makes it necessary that the men must be highly paid and specially trained."[55]

The short, nomadic careers of professional footballers differentiated players from other workers at the end of the nineteenth century. Typically, footballers did not work in their native towns, but were signed by teams great distances away. Moreover, as players were liable to be transferred, there could be no certainty as to where they would reside for the duration of their playing careers.

Football Players Magazine contained complaints of inadequate housing in cities where players had been hired. Scottish players were particularly upset by relocation.[56] While relatively high wages lured many players great distances, monetary compensation was not always sufficient to induce professionals to work on distant soil. The separation from families and friends, the general uprooting of their lives, and the recognition of the realities of professional football work terms and conditions prompted many to return to their native districts. The realization that professional football was perhaps an overly glamorized profession can be measured by the number of Scottish players who returned to Scotland from England to be "whitewashed" (reinstated as amateurs after having played professionally in England). After the 1890–1891 season, 115 Scotsmen were "whitewashed," and 73 more returned to Scotland the following year.[57]

Nevertheless, the practice of recruiting professional players from distant and diverse areas of Great Britain continued through the early part of the twentieth century, as Table 2 indicates. The distribution of players' home-towns in the Cup final of 1913 probably was typical of the many localities represented in other teams.[58]

TABLE 2
Hometowns of 1913 Cup Players

Aston Villa		Sunderland	
Player	Home Town	Player	Home Town
Hardy	Newbold	Butler	Lally Bank
Lyons	Hednesford	Gladwin	Worksop
Weston	Halesowen	Ness	Scarborough
Barber	West Stanley	Cuggy	Walker
Harrop	Heeley	Thompson	Prestonpans
Leach	Newcastle	Low	Aberdeen
Wallace	Sunderland	Mordue	Edmondsley
Halse	Leytonstone	Buchan	Plumstead
Hampton	Wellington	Richardson	Seaham Harbour
Stephenson	New Delaval	Holley	Glasgow
Bache	Stourbridge	Martin	Selston

Supporters of the amateur position during the controversy over profession-alism had complained of the "importation" of players from well outside a club's district. Critics of professionalism noted that the famous Preston North End sides of the 1880s each included nine Scotsmen. Other teams from Lancashire had scarcely more local representation: the Bolton Wan-derers comprised one Bolton native, four Welshmen, and five Scottish players; Great Lever had one man from its district playing with six Scottish players and a Welsh player; and the Burnley F.C. fielded seven starters who hailed from Scotland.[59] In 1884, a Birmingham writer asked pointedly whether there could be any "honour" in a "team of Scotchmen carrying the National Cup to any Lancashire village?"[60]

Small, local football clubs lost most of their native talent to larger professional teams, negating much of the significance of the geographic designations given to clubs. Skilled players gravitated to larger organizations that offered relatively high wages, as the experience of the Turton F.C.

showed. Players born in Turton left the town and eventually attained inter-League honors with wealthier clubs. A writer wondered whether it was consoling for Turton residents to know that "their offsprings are making a name for themselves in the higher walks of football life."[61] Arthur Bridgett thought the youth of Sunderland would "do better to support their own local clubs" than to sign outside the district. He acknowledged that young players were "doubtless tempted by the dangling of money bags, but the golden bait does not always turn out for the best."[62] In Bolton, one writer sought "more generous encouragement for youths of the neighborhood" to remain with local teams.[63]

The maturation of the football business created a contingent of men who worked at the game for a wage. They were employed for as long as they were perceived to benefit their company, much the way other workers were hired. Their backgrounds and the terms and conditions of their employment were in many respects similar to those of other workers. If their pay was higher, this in no way changed the basic relationship of professional football players to their employers. "Football is nowadays largely, though not primarily, a business," declared a writer, "and the playing of it a trade."[64]

By the turn of the century, considerable tension existed within the football business. Players and directors each sought to further their respective interests by acting in concert against the other party. Bitter disputes concerning the rights and welfare of each appeared in the sporting press as a complement to everyday reports of matches. By 1909, strife between players and the football hierarchy almost pre-empted the League season entirely, as cancellation of the schedule was averted by a truce arranged on the evening prior to the start of the season.

The possibility of such militant action among football players was raised with the spread of professionalism, itself a product of the game's commercialization. With the commercialization of football and the incorporation by team directors of the prevalent business techniques and relationships of late nineteenth century bourgeois society, confrontations became inevitable.

Notes

1. *Athletic News,* 15 March 1909, p. 4.
2. See, for example, the *Athletic News,* 28 August 1893.
3. *Athletic News*, 4 May, 1896.
4. *Cricket and Football Field,* 4 January, 1890, p. 4.
5. *Athletic News,* 30 April 1900, p. 1.
6. *Athletic News,* 19 Oct. 1903, p. 4.
7. The Master-Servant Act Revision of 1867, for instance, reduced penalties for strikers.
8. *Football's Who's Who* (London: C. Arthur Pearson, 1902), p. 126.
9. *Athletic News,* 12 Sept. 1910, p. 1.
10. *Cricket and Football Field,* 5 June 1909, p. 9.
11. *Athletic Journal,* 20 Nov. 1888, p. 4.

12. *Football and Sports Special,* 26 Aug. 1909, p. 6.

13. *Sports and Play,* 7 Jan. 1890, p. 735.

14. *Athletic News,* 30 March 1891, p. 3.

15. *Athletic News,* 14 Dec. 1891, p. 4.

16. *Athletic News,* 20 Feb. 1905, p. 1.

17. *Athletic News,* 31 Oct. 1883, p. 1.

18. *Cricket and Football Field,* 12 June 1909, p. 2.

19. *Football Annual* (Manchester), 1900, p. 13.

20. *Football Annual,* 1891, p. 53.

21. *Athletic News,* 10 October, 1883, p. 1.

22. *Athletic News,* 1 November 1882, p. 5.

23. *Athletic News,* 18 Dec. 1911, p. 1.

24. *Athletic News,* 18 Sept. 1888, p. 1.

25. *Athletic News,* 26 Aug. 1889, p. 1.

26. *Athletic News,* 26 Jan. 1886, p. 1.

27. *Midland Athletic Star,* 23 Oct. 1883, p. 5.

28. *Cricket and Football Field,* 5 Aug. 1899, p. 2.

29. *Football and Sports Special,* 15 May 1909, p. 5.

30. A. L. Bowley, *Wages and Income in the United Kingdom Since 1860* (Cambridge: 1937), p. 42.

31. *Athletic News,* 4 Nov. 1901, p. 4.

32. *Athletic News,* 23 Dec. 1889, p. 1.

33. *Athletic News,* 21 Dec. 1886, p. 1.

34. Cf. *Cricket and Football Field,* 10 Jan. and 11 April 1914.

35. *Cricket and Football Field,* 13 March 1909, p. 2.

36. *Athletic Journal,* 23 Oct. 1888, p. 19.

37. *Football and Sports Special,* 13 Feb. 1909, p. 5.

38. *Derby and Chesterfield Reporter* (Derby), 3 Jan. 1890, p. 2.

39. *Football Mail* (Hartlepool), 7 March 1914, p. 1.

40. Peter Morris, *West Bromwich Albion: Soccer in the Black Country* (London: Heinemann, 1965), pp. 34–35.

41. *Football and Sports Special,* 14 Aug. 1909, p. 3.

42. *Cricket and Football Field,* 23 Jan. 1909, p. 1.

43. *Athletic News,* 9 Oct. 1893, p. 1.

44. *Football Mail* (Newcastle), 13 Feb. 1904, p. 1.

45. *Athletic News,* 29 Jan. 1894, p. 1.

46. Wray Vamplew "Playing for Pay: The Earnings of Professional Sportsmen in England 1870–1914," paper to the Conference on the Making of Sporting Traditions, University of New South Wales, July 1979, p. 19.

47. *Cricket and Football Field,* 31 July 1909, p. 3.

48. *Football Players Magazine* (Manchester), Feb., 1914, p. 11.

49. Ernest Ensor, "The Football Madness," *Contemporary Review* (London), Nov. 1898, p. 755.

50. *Railway Review* (London), 20 Aug. 1909, p. 8.

51. *Cricket and Football Field,* 24 Jan. 1909, p. 2.

52. *The Times* (London), 2 May, 1914, p. 15.

53. *Northern Athlete,* 6 Sept. 1909, p. 2.

54. *Northern Athlete,* 6 Sept. 1909, p. 2.

55. *Football Players Magazine,* Feb. 1914, p. 11.

56. Cf. *Football Players Magazine,* Jan. 1913.

57.   Cf. *Athletic News,* 9 May 1892, and Sept. 1892.

58.   Home towns are listed as they were in the *Athletic News,* of 31 March 1913, without reference to county.

59.   N. L. Jackson, *Association Football* (London: George Newnes, 1899), p. 102.

60.   *The Athlete,* 6 Oct. 1884, p. 650.

61.   *Athletic News,* 11 March 1901, p. 1.

62.   *Sports Argus,* 31 July 1909, p. 4.

63.   *Cricket and Football Field,* 23 Jan. 1909, p. 4.

64.   *Cricket and Football Field,* 14 Aug. 1909, p. 8.

MORAL.—A "King" may be knocked down in various ways. If we were a "King" we would prefer that the blow came from another than a football quarter.

The link between football and other enterprises is illustrated in this cartoon from the *Liverpool Review* of 1892, which depicts the toppling of Everton F.C. director John Houlding. Generating auxiliary income through such enterprises as refreshment sales became a primary objective for clubs and occasionally was a point of disagreement among directors. *(courtesy The British Library, Colindale)*

Working-class spectators, who predominated at matches, usually stood and watched from uncovered terraces. *(courtesy BBC Hulton Picture Library)*

Billy Meredith (l.), from a Welsh coal mining community, typified the working-class origins of most professional footballers. A brilliant athlete, Meredith was active in representing his colleagues during the 1909 strike crisis. *(courtesy BBC Hulton Picture Library)*

SIGNING-ON SEASON.

In response to the request of the War Office Football Clubs are doing everything possible to accelerate Army recruiting.

The hierarchies of the Football League and Football Association stressed the many uses to which football could be put: teams could provide healthy manpower for the armed services and aid in recruitment drives. *(courtesy The British Library, Colindale)*

Recreational preferences usually were determined by factors of class, and football was unmistakably "the pastime of the poor." *(courtesy The British Library, Colindale)*

THE SHOOTING SEASON.

The Pastime of the Poor. | The Sport of the Squire.

Crystal Palace accommodated close to 100,000 for the annual Association Cup final. *(courtesy BBC Hulton Picture Library)*

CHAPTER SIX

Players Versus Directors

The fundamental business principle that an entrepreneur could retain a "controlling hand during such time as his capital is invested"[1] applied in football after about 1880. Often repeated in club memoranda of association, this principle defined the framework for labor relations within the football business. As directors controlled team finances, they sought, often against the wishes of players, to control labor.

While the rights of ownership were generally respected by players, the prerogatives of owner control contributed to considerable turbulence. Individual players expressed their dissatisfaction with the terms and conditions of football employment, and in 1907, professional players joined together to form a union to protect their interests. By 1909, directors confronted players who threatened to strike Football League matches and who had affiliated themselves with the General Federation of Trades Unions, a Trades Union Congress body. During the strike crisis of 1909, players also began to consider ways of conducting the game without investors, whose control, they felt, had made conditions unbearable.

Employer-employee relationships in football were unique in many respects. The transfer system and the Maximum Wage Rule inhibited the exercise of freedom of contract accorded employees in other fields. Although wages were higher than the industrial norm, careers were shorter in football than in other jobs. But while labor relations in the football business were somewhat special, professional players related to team directors as did other workingmen to their employers. Players recognized their interests to be separate and distinct from those of committeemen. The implementation of the transfer system and the wage maximum reflected a divergence of interests that contributed to bitter wage negotiations, strikes, and disputes over the rights of players. The objectives of directors and players were comparable to the goals of employers and employees in society as a whole.

A primary determinant of labor relations in football was the retreat by team owners from a philosophy of laissez-faire. This retreat took the form of legislation which was restrictive to players and which helped maintain team owner control of the football business. Thus, the implementation of the transfer system in 1890 effectively halted a player's freedom to negotiate simultaneously with more than one club. For instance, the system "deterred" Stoke City "and other clubs" from bargaining with Derby County F.C. professionals in 1890.[2] Davie Russell, a player for Preston North End, hoped to play for the Stoke City F.C. even though he was not dissatisfied with his wages in Preston. Stoke City applied to North End for Russell's release, but William Sudell, the Preston chairman, "refused it, as, under the circumstances, he has every right to do."[3] Sudell's "right" derived from Football League Rule 18, wherein the terms of the transfer system had been stipulated.

Players reacted with anger and frustration to the transfer system. The loss of their favored position in what had been a free and open market had made clear to many players that they needed a union or association, but during the 1890s, protests against the new system were conducted by individuals without the support of a collective body. Players adopted techniques such as "playing for one's papers" to gain release from a team. According to this strategy, players would give less than their best efforts on the field so that directors would send them elsewhere. Peter Morris noted that this ploy was used by West Bromwich Albion players in the 1890s.[4]

Another technique for acquiring release required the cooperation between a player and the club for which he hoped to play. A wage dispute between Holt and his employers, the Everton F.C. directorate, inspired Holt to offer the owners a "big sum" for his release. "It would appear," surmised one writer, "that some prominent club is anxious to secure his services" and had supplied the player with the money with which the offer was made.[5] This seems to have been a relatively isolated incident, as clubs that were eager to acquire a player could deal directly with the team that owned him. Players generally were unsuccessful in their individual attempts to secure release from teams. W. Gibson, for instance, tried repeatedly to obtain clearance from the Sunderland F.C. and, when denied, "left town without it, and has not been seen in the neighbourhood since."[6]

Davie Russell's experience at Preston illustrated that wages were not the only factor that players weighed when they sought release. Crompton, a Blackburn Rover player, sought transfer to Everton, although he was paid the maximum wage allowed. By contrast, players frequently were released when they wished to remain with their clubs. An article in the *Liverpool Review* in 1888 led inadvertently to the transfer of N. J. Ross, a fine player and strategist for the Liverpool F.C. The writer maintained that Ross, with his expertise and experience, should manage the team. This proposal offended the Liverpool committee, and Ross was handed his papers shortly after the article appeared.[7]

Investors expected that players would exercise no control over the way in which they performed their jobs. John Lewis' assertion that a player could take no initiative in deciding which position he was to play reflected this view, as did reports of player suspensions for refusal to follow the orders of the executive. The case of W. Davies, who was described as a "prominent Bolton player," provides a closer look at the occupational relationships

within the football business. Davies was suspended after insisting on following his own training schedule. When called before the Bolton F.C. committee, he "expressed the intention to go his own way and practically defied
the men who were paying his wages."[8] The *Athletic News* writer seemed
shocked that a player would presume to control any aspect of his labor and
would react to his employer in such a defiant manner.

As the owner's power grew, some players recognized the need for a union
to protect their interests, and the adoption of the transfer system raised the
possibility of a collective response among players. After noting that professionals were "still to be denied the privilege of free contract," a player on
the Everton F.C. sent a letter to the *Athletic News* urging the formation of a
players association:

> I have been speaking to several men in my own and other teams, and we have
> come to the conclusion that we will not have [the transfer system]; and, if it is
> insisted upon we will at once combine in a union of our own for protection and
> justice. . . .
>
> I do not advocate the breaking of contracts, but I emphatically demand the
> same freedom to engage for the coming season that the League claims for
> itself. . . . We ask for nothing but that our terms and freedom of contract will not
> be interfered with by the League in future, and if they attempt it then I cry,
> "Hurrah! for union and justice!"

The Everton player also expressed the frustrations that others felt regarding
their working conditions and brief tenure as professionals. In the same letter,
he hoped that players would openly express their dissatisfaction with

> greedy, grasping committees. We draw the gates; give the sport, and turn out in
> all weathers, be it rain, hail, frost, or snow in our bare heads, and thin covering.
> We are expected to turn up, and play up, and do our best to please crowd, critic,
> and committee. We run the risk of getting maimed for life, and if any of us are
> fortunate enough to escape, then in three or four seasons we are called old
> crocks, treated like a broken one, and simply thrown aside.[9]

Fears of reprisal for being associated with unionism and the rapid changes in
personnel among players made organization difficult. The unstated rule was
that players could—and in time would —be replaced, and there was no point
in hastening the process. In reporting a tentative effort at union organization
in 1893, a writer commented that "only the wilder spirits" believed that
players "could be masters of the situation."[10] The competition for jobs and
relatively good wages functioned as a brake to militancy for close to a
decade.

Mention of a players' union was made in January 1899 issues of *Athletic
News*, but it was not discussed further in the press after 1900. Cliff Lloyd,
current secretary of the present-day Players' Union, the organization that
succeeded this original body, found no records of the earlier union. The fact
that only a few references to the first union were made might be a reflection of
its slight impact. It had as its goals a campaign against the transfer system as

well as the presentation of player grievances before the Football Association while also engaging in benevolent work on behalf of players.

Derek Dougan and Percy Young have asserted that the Football Association and the Football League hoped that "by playing their cards right they could defeat the threat of a Union."[11] They were evidently referring to numerous proposals submitted by directors who advocated the abolition of the Maximum Wage Rule. As an end to restrictions seemed possible between 1901 and 1908, it was conceivable that players who might otherwise have joined the union, in the hope that organized player resistance could be effective, refrained from doing so. By waiting for repeal of the wage maximum through director initiative, the union encouraged the view that the football hierarchy itself could improve the players' lot. Rather than taking independent action on behalf of players, the secretary of the union devoted his energies to individual player grievances, such as the Sanderson versus Notts County dispute over back wages. While in this instance the case was adjudicated in favor of the player, the union failed to press for the abolition of financial restraints that adversely affected all players. During the course of inconclusive debates among owners over the abolition of restrictions, the first players union passed out of existence, presumably for lack of player support. It was not until 1907 that a militant and independent union emerged in its place.

As its name implied, the Players Union and Benefit Society functioned as a friendly society and represented players before management. A 5 s. entrance fee and 6 d. weekly dues were asked of the professionals of the Football League, the Southern League, and the Lancashire Combination who formed the bulk of the Union's membership.

Various proposals concerning player representation within the Union were discussed during December 1907. Charlie Roberts, a player for Manchester United, proposed at the inaugural meeting of the Union that each team send a representative. This proposal was withdrawn, and an alternate plan for regional representation was approved pending further growth in membership.[12] By 15 December 1908, at the first annual general meeting, a revised representation plan permitted thirty Football League clubs, nineteen Southern League clubs, and one Lancashire Combination Club to sponsor one delegate each. In order to qualify to send a representative, a club was required to have twelve union members whose dues were fully paid. Immediately prior to the general meeting of 1908, more than 1,300 players from seventy teams had joined the Union.

The rapid growth in membership was in part attributed to the benevolent work undertaken by the Union during the first year of its existence. On 1 April 1908, the Union instructed its secretary to contact the Sheffield United F.C. to see if they would increase their donation to the parents of a recently deceased player. The Union sent the family £20.[13] In a November 1908 meeting the Union decided to send £10 to the widow of former player George Smith, and, at the same meeting, £7 10s. were delivered to

F. Thompson, a former player who was "in destitute circumstances."[14] At the 1908 annual general meeting, it was resolved that each player would donate one shilling to a burial fund upon the death of a member.

The Players' Union was also enterprising in representing its membership in disputes with the various professional leagues and clubs. The Union's efforts in the case of two professionals in their suit against the Crystal Palace F.C. helped demonstrate that professional football players were "workmen" within the definition of the Workmens Compensation Act of 1906, and numerous considerations under the act subsequently were granted to players. In an advertisement in its own journal, *Football Players Magazine,* the Union listed as an advantage of membership its participation in "all cases on behalf of players." If a player needed help, but couldn't afford it, the Union would "assist him with legal advice quite free." And the Union had a good record: it had "already won sixty cases."[15] In September 1914, W. G. Domleo forwarded to the Players' Union an additional contribution after the Union's solicitor, Thomas Hinchcliffe, induced the Bury F.C. to pay Domleo £60 and legal costs. Domleo stated that the settlement would not have been made "if you had not taken it up for me."[16] The November 1913 issue of *Football Players Magazine* contained four letters from players whose cases had been settled through Union intervention.

Perhaps the most compelling reason to join the Players' Union was the Union's determination to abolish all restrictive financial legislation in the football business. On 16 September 1908, at a Union Management Committee meeting in Manchester, representatives affirmed that the abolition of all restrictions on the financial relations of players with their clubs "is the only satisfactory solution to the wages problem." The Union stated that it would simultaneously welcome "any movement tending to improve the financial conditions" of its members.[17] This resolution was echoed on 15 December 1908, at the annual general meeting where players sought the solution of the "wages problem" in the "abolition of all restrictions." For the policy of limitation and restriction, the Union proposed a "policy of mutual agreement, based on free bargaining, in all matters affecting the service of players and their clubs."[18] Players reaffirmed their desire to eliminate financial restrictions two years later when the Football Association distributed circulars asking whether professionals favored the abolition of the wage maximum. A substantial number, 759 players, responded that they favored abolition, while 260 wished to retain the Maximum Wage Rule.[19]

By 1909, financial restriction and the right of the Players' Union to contest contractual restraints were sufficiently pressing issues to arouse considerable militancy among professionals. Ironically, players demanded little more than the application of those laissez-faire principles which had been rallying points for the middle classes in the early and middle decades of the nineteenth century. "In asking for freedom of contract," players were "only asking what some of the leading clubs in the League are asking."[20] The position of football professionals compared unfavorably to that of other workers with regard to their rights in the market place. "Even a crossing sweeper," complained one player, "has freedom of contract; this is denied us."[21]

Player determination to restore free market relationships in football elicited the support of some Liberals, who recognized that the principles at stake in the football controversy also applied to general policy. A writer in the *Eastern Daily Press,* a Liberal newspaper published in Norwich, argued that players were

> deprived of the legitimate chances of [their] profession. We have but to imagine similar restrictions in any trade or other occupation to realize how grossly unjust is the restriction on the salary. In the factory or the workshop a man may receive the highest salary that is considered an equivalent for his particular skill or merit; but in the football field no exceptional brilliancy of play will enable him to earn more than the fixed amount.[22]

Truth, a Liberal weekly published in London, warned that "if people like to employ men to play football for them they must take the ordinary risks of the business."[23] The traditional Liberal advocacy of free trade and the recognition of a working-class constituency, elsewhere reflected in the "Lib-Lab" electoral alliance, crystallized around matters of sports, as well. Nevertheless, professional footballers adopted the precepts of classical political economy at a time when laissez-faire was receiving less support from owners who, like other investors and economic theorists, now often favored intervention in the marketplace.

The players' call for the abolition of restrictive legislation probably was less a doctrinal or ideological point than it was a convenient way to publicize and secure their interests. Owners, too, adapted to various ideological currents as their needs required. The manner in which player and owner interests were pursued was reminiscent of many another labor dispute, and the issue of laissez-faire was a factor primarily as a ploy to enhance the positions of the contending parties.

In the 11 January 1909 issue of the *Athletic News,* C. E. Sutcliffe assayed the status of professional football team owners and players. In an article headlined, "Who Shall Be Masters? Players Or Clubs?", Sutcliffe asserted that players sought "all the wages, all the bonuses, and all the transfer fees they can get. If I am to write my honest opinion I must go further and say the players want to be masters."

Sutcliffe was concerned about what he considered to be the impending conflict between owners and players. As a member of the Burnley F.C. directorate and a director of the Football League, he was aware of the private communications among League owners regarding a proposal of amnesty for owners who had violated the Maximum Wage Rule. In February 1909, a month after Sutcliffe's column was printed, owners of Football League teams accepted an amnesty offer from the Football Association which forbade the prosecution of teams for past violations of the £4 wage limit. After the amnesty period football League directors promised to obey the Maximum Wage Rule and to cease illegal bidding for players. Such bidding had raised the salaries of some players to £7 per week and had tended to restore to players an advantage in the marketplace. Sutcliffe recognized the importance of the agreement and its effect on the constellation of forces within the football business: "It is now not a fight between one section of clubs and another, but whether the players have to rule the' clubs or the clubs the players."[24] A writer for *Cricket and Football Field* felt that a "crisis between the League and the Players' Union is nigh at hand" and that shortly "we shall wake up and find an open declaration of war."[25]

At the time of its proposal on 15 July 1908, the Football Association's amnesty offer added little to the dialogue concerning the maximum wage. The document itself was not acted upon by directors for more than five months, and it seems to have been accepted only after the Players' Union determined to challenge financial restrictions. "There can be no doubt," offered one writer, "that the clubs were influenced in their adoption [of amnesty] by the policy of the Players' Union."[26]

With the signing of the amnesty agreement, the Players' Union announced its intention of initiating legal proceedings against clubs that failed to compensate those players with whom preamnesty agreements had been made. Clubs informed the Football Association of the Union's course, and the Association indicated to the Union that "under the laws of the parent body [i.e., the Football Association], all such disputes must be adjudicated by it, and not be taken into a court of law."[27]

This decision, which in effect barred any outside arbitration between the Association and the players, added to a controversy that seemed to grow ever wider in scope. The *Athletic News* scolded players for their "defiance" of Football Association statutes which forbade recourse to any judicial system apart from that established within the Association. According to the *Athletic News,* the Players' Union was obliged to act under rules formulated by the "governing authority," the Football Association.[28]

The Players' Union contended that its members identified themselves as workingmen who were entitled to the same protection under the law given to other wage earners. The Football Association, the Football League, and the clubs, reasoned Union officials, had no special authority to prevent access to legal redress. Herbert Broomfield, secretary of the Players' Union, wrote that members of the Union Management Committee were not convinced that they were "expected to regard seriously the opinion that a football player forfeits a common legal right on entering into a professional engagement with a football club."[29] An official of the Union told the press that all his organization sought was "justice," and that it seemed

> absurd for the Football Association to usurp the functions of a judicial tribunal, and tell us that when a player cannot get fair and just treatment from his club we must not go to law to enforce his rights.[30]

As the playing season drew to a close in the spring of 1909, other developments intensified the hostility between owners and players. The Football Association prohibited the playing of an exhibition match, the receipts from which were to have been contributed to the players' benevolent fund. This decision inspired players to discuss whether they might conduct that game—and all future matches—independently of the Association, the League, or club directors.

During 7 May 1909 meeting of the Players' Union in Manchester, the Management Committee proposed to affiliate with the General Federation of Trades Unions (GFTU), a Trades Union Congress organization which helped to support striking workers in several trades. Affiliation might have been seen as an appropriate response to the developments of the preceding days, as the Football Association had ruled that officers and members of the Union Management Committee must "act in accordance with the rules of the Football Association" or they would be suspended from taking part in football or football management.[31]

The Union began to prepare for a strike. It was resolved that if the Union Management Committee should declare a strike, all Union members would receive £1 per week until a settlement could be reached.[32]

According to Football Association Minutes of 3 May 1909, owners perceived that the Union "sought to promote a strike" rather than work in "conformity with the rules of the Football Association." On 9 June, the Association extended its sanctions to all members of the Players' Union. After its previously unsuccessful attempt to alienate the Union Management Committee from the rank-and-file membership, the Association declared that all players would be required to terminate their membership in the Players' Union by 1 July or lose their registration with the Football Association. The loss of registration would have barred players from participation in League matches and thus would have deprived Union members of their livelihood as football players.[33]

William Pickford, an official of the Football Association, understood the significance of the wrangling between owners and players over the issues of restriction and control. He spoke for the owners when he stated that if it "comes down to the question of who is to be master, the clubs who pay the wages or the players who receive them, we must know where we are." Using one of the owners' most effective appeals for support from the football public, Pickford declared that, while the talk of a strike might sound plausible to some, he did not think it likely that the majority of football spectators would support a strike by highly paid athletes who only worked one afternoon per week.[34] This and other references by directors and sportswriters to salaries were designed to damage player efforts at gaining support for their cause. William McGregor wrote that he would "like to know what the bona-fide Trades Union working man thinks" of such well-paid people as footballers, who were so well remunerated for but an hour and a half's work, who travel in well-appointed saloons, having dinner and tea on board, and [who] are waited upon as if they were dukes or lords. . . . Then he has nearly four months holiday, and has £4 per week coming in all the time. I think most Trades Unionists would put up with the little grievances for such treatment.[35]

John Lewis wrote a column in which he expressed the same sentiments. He noted that professional football players received £4 a week, were treated to "no end of enjoyable outings," were allowed four months holiday per year, and were given a benefit match which provided additional income. Lewis declared that in contrasting their lots, "the average working man will say, and say rightly, that players are able to take care of themselves."[36]

One reason for the frequency of such comments was the concern of the football hierarchy with the state of public opinion. Players received considerable popular support in spite of the efforts of the owner-controlled press to alienate the public from professional footballers. While most sporting papers lauded the good sense of the "football public" for withholding its support from the Players' Union, writers were unable even to define this "football public." For most papers, "public opinion" seemed to coincide with what owners hoped would occur during the crisis.

One journal did state, with a twinge of disappointment, that the "workers of England" had promised their "sympathetic support" to the Players' Union,[37] and another admitted that the Union was "backed up" by the "bulk of public opinion."[38] Indeed, the Players' Union enjoyed the backing of the General Federation of Trades Unions as well as that other union and labor publications. The power of the GFTU was acknowledged in such pro-owner papers as *Cricket and Football Field,* whose editor speculated in the summer of 1909 that if the Federation "throws its entire weight into the scale on behalf of the men, half the professional clubs in the country will be bankrupt before the end of October."[39] The Lancashire and Cheshire Federation of Trade and Labour Councils, which represented thousands of trade unionists, notified the Players' Union that it would provide "such assistance as will enable that Union to withstand the attempts to crush it out of existence."[40] The Railwaymens Union also lent support to the players, and advised them that "with loyalty to themselves they can become free to combine as any person who at law is a 'workman.' " Players were "not novices in the art of organisation, and they know the powers that can be brought to bear."[41] Equally strong support came from the editors of the *Sheffield Guardian,* an organ of the Independent Labour party. This journal gave the dispute extensive coverage and maintained that "every Trade Unionist in the country worth his salt will be behind the Players' Union."[42]

The trade union support for professional football players in 1909 may well have been a reciprocal response to earlier instances in which footballers had played matches to raise money for other striking union members and their families. Even before the existence of a footballers' union, players had expressed their willingness to support fellow workingmen. In Bolton in 1887, for example, the Wanderers played an exhibition match to benefit striking engineers. Team members were willing to forego compensation "for the cause of the masses against the classes."[43] Similarly, in 1893, the willingness of Everton players to travel to Manchester to play a match for the benefit of operatives "who have been thrown out of work in the cotton trade" was noted in the *Athletic News*. The writer of the article commented further that there were many destitute families "to whom monetary assistance, however small, will be welcomed. . . . It is pleasing to know that football can be devoted to charitable purposes."[44]

Trade unionist support also derived in large part from the fundamental question of union rights posed in the football dispute. One trade's actions to prevent employees from exercising their rights was perceived as a threat to the entire labor movement. A writer for the *Railway Review* saw management's stand as a familiar and well-worn tactic by employers and discussed it in terms that had been applied to other labor struggles:

> To say that a player who signs an agreement to act within the rules of an association shall not exercise his right at common law is too feudalistic an argument. We have grown beyond this stage nowadays. That kind of argument has been crushed out in the railway service by force of Trade Unionism, and the football players with any sense of personal dignity will make an organised effort to clear the football area of such anachronistic rubbish.[45]

A writer in the *Sheffield Guardian* drew a comparison between football and more ordinary work. It was important for workingmen to support the players, he argued, because as the clubs had grown,

> there as been the same tendency to divorce the control of the game and its finances from the people who are actively engaged in and are the backbone of the sport, just as the control and finances of the industries of the nation are taken out of the hands of those who are the very life's blood of such industries. . . . [Footballers] are beginning to recognize that the only remedy for combatting the crushing tendencies of the dominating clique lies with themselves, and, so, like their confreres in the industrial world, they are uniting together and have formed a union to protect their interests.[46]

Players saw the structural similarity between the football business and other commercial concerns as the dispute brought to light the fundamental issue of control. The transfer system, the Maximum Wage Rule, and even the players' right to organize were problems generated by the basic framework which established wage labor as the mode through which football at its highest level was conceived. Team owners and players saw the retention or abolition of directorial control as the most important element of the crisis.

When owners withdrew their permission for the playing of a match to benefit the players' benevolent fund in the spring of 1909, professionals began contemplating the possibility of organizing matches by themselves, without directorial participation. In a memo to players that was printed in the *Football and Sports Special* in June, Union secretary Herbert Broomfield stated that owner attempts to "squash the Union" had placed professionals in a "position for striking a decisive blow for independence." The players on the better clubs in particular remained loyal to the Union, and Broomfield hoped to arrange matches with Manchester United and Newcastle United players as the core group around which the challenge to League owners could focus. "I shall not be a bit surprised if this does not mean a parting of the ways," Broomfield predicted, with reference to Union players and the Football League.[47] One of the Manchester United players, Billy Meredith, wrote a column in which he discussed the possibilities of a player strike and the arrangement of player-controlled matches.[48] An unnamed player, presumably from Newcastle, described how players could schedule engagements:

> We could play matches all over the country if we needed the money. What is to prevent our playing matches and [paying] a bonus for the winning team? We should have all the stars out, and with a bonus for a win, we could take £1,000 at every match.[49]

The response from the football hierarchy underlined the directors' intentions of preserving the relationships that had prevailed in professional football for the previous twenty years. William Pickford declared that when control of any sport by professionals exists, "it is almost invariably a bad thing."[50] At a meeting of the Football Association Council, Preston North End director Thomas Houghton vowed that "the clubs are not going to be dragged at the tail of the Players' Union,"[51] while the editor of the *Liverpool Fooball Echo* wrote, "Long live football—as it is governed at present. But death to any football which shall be player-managed."[52]

Owner resistance to player control was rooted in the desire to retain existing class relationships, a desire made explicit in numerous articles in which members of the football hierarchy were compared favorably to Union "upstarts." After admitting his ignorance of how well workers on the Lancashire and Yorkshire Railway had actually run the affairs of the Newton Heath F.C. some years before, a writer for the *Football and Sports Special* demurred that he had

> the highest respect for workingmen, and I like to see their representatives everywhere, but I cannot bring myself to believe in the possibility of a club run by working men directors. After all, men who are accustomed to conducting big business enterprises of their own are better fitted to conduct a big football enterprise—and a football club is a big business enterprise, indeed.[53]

The editor of *Cricket and Football Field* divined that the "great majority" of the game's supporters would "doubtless prefer" that football be conducted as it had been, "with men at the head who in the main have plenty of this world's goods and give their time and consideration to football's welfare as a diversion and as a tonic."[54] This statement was a diplomatic way of wording a message that was sharply stated when directed at players: professional footballers were "paid to play and leave the rest to the clubs."[55]

On the surface, owners were scornful of the players' talk of organizing their own matches. The editor of *Football and Sports Special* ridiculed a player tour as a "music hall turn" which was "too foolish to discuss." He felt that Broomfield had a "very much inflated conception of the public's estimation of what is sport," and he doubted that many would attend what he termed a "dumb show."[56] The *Athletic News* added that the "football public" was against the players, and the public,

> who have been educated up to the belief that only competition football is worth seeing . . . are not going to be gulled into patronising any hippodrome matches which these men may arrange among themselves.[57]

The comments of the editor of the *Northern Athlete* on player moves to organize their matches revealed how professional football had been promoted and publicized. He stated that the public certainly would ignore games between "non-descript teams, even though every man was an international."* Rather, it was the rivalry of town versus town, city versus city, "and the all important something at stake that has made the game."[58] However, the editor ignored the fact that teams which were located in a given town or city generally did not sign up natives of their districts, so that the "rivalry of town versus town" was in team name only. Moreover, he failed to amplify his notion of the "all important something," which conceivably was nothing more than the artificially induced hoopla and hysteria attendant to big-time sports. Present-day sports critics have analyzed this phenomenon,[59] which nineteenth-century observers had just begun to perceive. The remarks of the editor from Newcastle recall Football Association Vice-President N. L. Jackson's comments about the "factitious interest" in matches created by the sporting press.[60]

Owners and sportwriters grew more antagonistic as the Union position remained firm throughout the summer of 1909, and players were depicted in the press as greedy killjoys whose actions were inexplicable except in terms of avariciousness. John Lewis claimed to speak for "thousands of club supporters" who, he claimed, would "rejoice at the opportunity of getting rid of four-pound-a-weekers who give nothing like value for their money."[61] A writer for the *Athletic News* insisted that the "greed and avarice" of the professionals would doom player-controlled football and would simultaneously cause the community to "revolt from the game."[62]

Much of the militancy of the players' stand was attributed to the influence of malcontents who swayed otherwise satisfied employees. The football hierarchy found it hard to understand that players saw their interests as distinct from those of the owners; furthermore, they were astonished that players would act in order to secure their interests or that they could conceive of a different balance of power between themselves and the owners. The press began a campaign berating Union leaders in order to create divisions

---

*An international is an exceptionally talented player selected to represent England, Scotland, Ireland, or Wales in specially arranged annual matches.

among footballers. The vast majority of professionals would "recognize that their best friends are the Football Association—but they have been led away by disappointed men who have nursed their grievances until they have become agitators."[63] James Grant, treasurer of the Liverpool Football Association, felt that "firebrands" were "dangerous and should be kept well under control or they will injure the body with which they are associated."[64] Moreover, added another writer, if players failed to understand the hierarchy's position, it was the result of the "farrago of nonsense" served up by the Union:

> Let us look at the position in a dispassionate manner. We use these words because the Players' Union does not seem to possess a calm, clear vision of the situation.[65]

In another article, players were instructed to write, "in all penitence," to the Association asking for the removal of their suspension after resigning from the Union.[66]

The press simultaneously sought to delineate a role for the Union which writers and club directors deemed suitable. William McGregor felt that there was indeed room for a Players' Union, but that such an orgnization should concern itself with reducing "rough play" on the pitch and "endeavouring to make the calling of the professional footballer as high-toned as possible."[67] James Grant exclaimed, "By all means let us have a Players' Union," and then qualified his remark by adding, "but let it work in unison with and not in opposition to the powers that be."[68] J. C. Clegg and Sir William Clegg, who had served as directors on Sheffield clubs and were prominent in Football Association affairs, maintained that the hierarchy was not opposed to trade unionism in principle. Their statements on the subject elicited a response from the *Sheffield Guardian,* whose editor compared the Cleggs to the

> employer who is favourable to trade unionism so long as it doesn't do anything he doesn't want. But let it touch his interest, and the devil take it.[69]

As news of strike threats and player suspensions filled the pages of the sporting press, writers often posed as objective observers and spokesmen for the "football public," offering solutions which were in fact no more than restatements of the proposals of club management committees. On other occasions, writers made sentimental pleas to the professionals, urging them not to let the "thousands of people who are anxiously waiting for the season to start suffer a disappointment through the action of a few dissatisfied players."[70] Still another approach taken by the press focused on threats that striking players would never again find employment in professional football. "We may take it for granted," warned the *Cricket and Football Field,* "that the player who strikes has finished his earning capacity as a footballer."[71] A writer in the *Northern Athlete* stated baldly that players were "in the wrong, and will have to climb down for good—or quit."[72] This mixture of a humble appeal as well as a more abusive approach was directed at players by the game's governors through their ties to the sporting press.

There are little data available regarding the support that the Union received from professional players on a daily basis between May and the middle of August 1909. While the Football Association had ordered all professionals to resign from the Players' Union, it is impossible to tabulate the number of those who followed the Association's mandate, as Union membership lapsed automatically after 30 April, and was not again solicited until the end of the summer. Moreover, the leadership interpreted the absence of visible support for the Union during the early months of the close-season as necessary if players were to continue to receive summer wages from their clubs. Union leaders reasoned that nothing could be gained by antagonizing the clubs or the Association before the season commmenced: the critical period for support would be at the start of the next campaign, and the "promises from the leading players to rejoin at the beginning of the next season" were encouraging to the Union leadership.[73]

To be sure, the Union never attained the active support of each and every professional football player. One reason, as a critic of the Union suggested, was that most workers, including footballers, would be satisfied merely with a higher than average wage:

> To think that these young gentlemen who are earning £4 per week all the year round will return home and ask to do a week's work of 48 hours at something like their former remuneration of 30 s., or less, will cause a lot of amusement amongst football people generally.[74]

The satisfaction of some footballers with a relatively high wage was analogous to the focus of the "labor aristocracy" on purely economic gains.

Some players who may have approved of the Union position refrained from joining for fear of reprisal. The desire to postpone for as long as possible the inevitable return to their nonfootball work no doubt prompted a good number of players to withhold active support for a strike, although they considered the issues worth striking for. *Truth* stated that professionals who had "not joined the Union" but who were "in sympathy with it" played a significant role in the resolution of the crisis.[75]

The Management Committee of the Players' Union adopted a stance that went beyond the discussion of wages and directly to the heart of the issue of control. The Management Committee included luminaries from Manchester United, Middlesbrough, and Newcastle United. Their teammates were regarded to be among the more militant footballers, although the press was inclined to underestimate militancy and player support for the Union. The *Newcastle Weekly Chronicle* noted as early as 12 June 1909, that the Players' Union "received its quietus at the hands of the Football Association.[76] Just one week later, with the most heated events of the strike crisis still months away, the *Liverpool Football Echo* made reference to the Union as if it were no longer in existence.[77] J. A. H. Catton of the *Athletic News* suggested that players from most Football League teams were not supportive of the Union's position, and he mentioned players on the Everton F.C. as being among those who would be unwilling to strike. Nevertheless, only a few players notified the Football Association that they intended to resign from the Union, and a somewhat cautious approach characterized the attitudes of most players throughout most of the summer.

Summer wages were withheld from the players, and they did not practice during the training period in August. Meanwhile, the campaign against militant players continued in the press. As the regular season approached, many players indicated their refusal to resign from the Union. A writer for the *Newcastle Weekley Chronicle* noted that the Sunderland team "to a man" decided to rejoin the Union and that "should the Football Association persist in their desire to suspend all players who become members of the Union, a very serious situation will arise."[78]

The same Everton F.C. players whom Catton had praised, recognized the necessity of expressing their position when the opening match of the season was less than two weeks away. In a joint letter, addressed by twenty-two Everton players to their directors, the players declared:

> Having in mind the suspension and refusal to pay the back wages to our colleague Coleman, and the players of Manchester United, whom we all recognize as being the means of enabling the Union to exist, we absolutely refuse to allow these men to suffer any punishment or to leave them in the lurch.[79]

Each player enclosed a postard notifying the directors of his renewed Union membership. "Much anxiety" was reported by one journalist "among the officials of certain clubs as to how many of their men have actually rejoined the Players' Union."[80] As the season approached and tensions mounted, the Union claimed the active support of players on the Bolton, Bury, Manchester City, Sunderland, Liverpool, and Everton teams in addition to the nucleus of Manchester United, Middlesbrough, and Newcastle United players. In late August, representatives of Aston Villa, Birmingham City, and West Bromwich Albion were addressed by Union executive secretary Herbert Broomfield, and it was "unanimously decided by the fifty players present to support the Players' Union."[81]

The perceived importance of a strike in professional football and its relation to labor disputes in other industries was occasionally reflected in the press. A writer for *Cricket and Football Field* recognized that football was much more than just a sport when he wrote:

> [L]arge employers of trade union labour are to be found on the directorate of nearly every professional club in the country, so that if the Federation of Trades Unions acts with spirit it will not only bring about the ruin of football "gates," but precipitate serious labour troubles all over the country. With this aspect of the case revealed, the dispute becomes one of national importance, and it should therefore engage the immediate attention of the very highest authorities.[82]

As preparations to cancel opening day matches were undertaken, owners offered a truce to players pending the fulfillment of scheduled matches. At a hastily called meeting on the eve of the season's inaugural games, players accepted the truce when they were assured that their basic grievances—wages, the transfer system, and the right to union representation—would be considered in the course of a negotiations schedule.

A compromise between owners and players was reached three months later. According to this agreement, the Players' Union dropped its affiliation with the GFTU. The players also were assured that the Football Association Council would "continue to press for the removal of the financial arrangements from the rules,"[83] while the Players' Union was recognized by the Football Association. Suspensions which had arisen out of the dispute were lifted, and back wages due players during their suspensions were ordered paid.

Another vital issue concerned Workmen's Compensation benefits. The Football Association allowed in the agreement that Workmen's Compensation cases could proceed through the courts and would not be adjudicated at special hearings conducted by the Association. All claims and disputes between clubs and players initially would be heard by the Association; however, if either party were dissatisfied with the decision, it had the right to bring the case to court.

The events of 1909 vindicated the self-perceptions of players as workingmen, although the settlement regarding Workmen's Compensation only stated in legal terms conditions that had prevailed since the inception of the football business. With the formation of a successful players' union, footballers grew more discerning and militant. They had graduated from engaging in isolated, individual actions of protest; they had experienced the difficulties inherent in organizing a union that had failed to represent player interests independently; and, by 1909, they had realized the need for militant action to secure their interests.

Notes

1. *Athletic News,* 16 March 1903, p. 1.
2. *Derby and Derbyshire Gazette* (Derby), 17 Jan. 1890, p. 3.
3. *Athletic News,* 3 Feb. 1890, p. 1.
4. Morris, *West Bromwich Albion,* p. 26.
5. *Athletic News,* 7 Sept. 1891, p. 1.
6. *Athletic News,* 28 Dec. 1891, p. 2.
7. Percy M. Young, *Football on Merseyside,* (London: Stanley Paul, 1963), pp. 30–31.
8. *Athletic News,* 16 Dec. 1899, p. 1.
9. *Athletic News,* 20 April 1891, p. 7.
10. *Athletic News,* 9 Oct. 1893, p. 1.
11. Derek Dougan and Percy M. Young, *On the Spot: Football As A Profession,* (London: Stanley Paul, 1974), p. 44.
12. Professional Footballers Association Minutes, 1907.

13. Professional Footballers Association Minutes, 1908.

14. Professional Footballers Association Minutes, 1908.

15. *Football Players Magazine,* Oct. 1913, p. 15.

16. *Football Players Magazine,* Sept. 1913, p. 13.

17. Professional Footballers Association Minutes, 1908.

18. Professional Footballers Association Minutes, 1908.

19. *Athletic News,* 24 Jan. 1910, p. 1.

20. *Football and Sports Special,* 16 Jan. 1909, p. 3.

21. *Athletic News,* 20 April 1891, p. 7.

22. *Eastern Daily Press* (Norwich), 19 Oct. 1903, p. 9.

23. *Truth* (London, 8 Sept. 1909, p. 579.

24. *Athletic News,* 11 Jan. 1909, p. 4.

25. *Cricket and Football Field,* 16 Jan. 1909, p. 1.

26. *Football and Sports Special,* 13 Feb. 1909, p. 3.

27. Football Association Minutes, 1909.

28. *Athletic News,* 15 March 1909, p. 1.

29. *Athletic News,* 22 Feb. 1909, p. 4.

30. *Cricket and Football Field,* 13 March 1909, p. 1.

31. Football Association Minutes, 1909.

32. Footballers Association Minutes, 1909.

33. Football Association Minutes, 1909.

34. *Athletic News,* 9 Aug. 1909, p. 1.

35. *Sports Argus,* 28 Aug. 1909, p. 1.

35. *Sports Argus,* 28 Aug. 1909, p. 1.

36. *Football and Sports Special,* 13 March 1909, p. 4.

37. *Northern Athlete,* 2 Aug. 1909, p. 2.

38. *Liverpool Football Echo,* 14 Aug. 1909, p. 3.

39. *Cricket and Football Field,* 28 Aug. 1909, p. 8.

40. *Cricket and Football Field,* 7 Aug. 1909, p. 1.

41. *Railway Review,* 20 Aug. 1909, p. 8.

42. *Sheffield Guardian,* 23 July 1909, p. 3.

43. *Cricket and Football Field,* 3 Sept. 1887, p. 2.

44. *Athletic News,* 6 Feb. 1893, p. 1.

45. *Railway Review,* 16 July 1909, p. 8.

46. *Sheffield Guardian,* 23 April 1909, p. 2.

47. *Football and Sports Special,* 26 June 1909, p. 4.

48. *Football and Sports Special* 17 July 1909, p. 5.

49. *Northern Athlete,* 28 June 1909, p. 1.

50. *Football Echo (Sunderland),* 4 Sept. 1909, p. 1.

51. *Cricket and Football Field,* 5 June 1909, p. 1.

52. *Liverpool Football Echo,* 12 June 1909, p. 1.

53. *Football and Sports Special,* 3 April 1909, p. 4.

54. *Cricket and Football Field,* 21 Aug. 1909, p. 1.

55. *Football and Sports Special,* 26 Aug. 1909, p. 6.

56. *Football and Sports Special,* 3 July 1909, p. 1.

57. *Athletic News,* 12 July 1909, p. 1.

58. *Northern Athlete,* 28 June 1909, p. 1.

59. See, for instance, Paul Hoch, *Rip Off The Big Game: The Exploitation of Sports by the Power Elite* (Garden City: Doubleday, 1972).

60.   *Pastime,* 10 April 1889, p. 222.
61.   *Football and Sports Special,* 20 March 1909, p. 4.
62.   *Athletic News,* 28 June 1909, p. 1.
63.   *Athletic News,* 2 Aug. 1909, p. 1.
64.   *Cricket and Football Field,* 5 June 1909, p. 9.
65.   *Athletic News,* 15 March 1909, p. 1.
66.   *Athletic News,* 12 July, 1909, p. 1.
67.   *Football Echo (Sunderland),* 27 March 1909, p. 1.
68.   *Cricket and Football Field,* 5 June 1909, p. 9.
69.   *Sheffield Guardian,* 30 July 1909, p. 3.
70.   *Cricket and Football Field,* 21 August 1909, p. 1.
71.   *Cricket and Football Field,* 19 June 1909, p. 3.
72.   *Northern Athlete,* 19 July 1909, p. 3.
73.   *Cricket and Football Field,* 17 July 1909, p. 11.
74.   *Football and Sports Special,* 3 July 1909, p. 1.
75.   *Truth,* 8 September 1909, p. 578.
76.   *Newcastle Weekly Chronicle,* 12 June 1909, p. 1.
77.   *Liverpool Football Echo,* 19 June 1909, p. 1.
78.   *Newscastle Weekly Chronicle,* 14 Aug. 1909, p. 1.
79.   *Athletic News,* 6 Sept. 1909, p. 1.
80.   *Newcastle Weekly Chronicle,* 26 Aug. 1909, p. 8.
81.   *Newcastle Weekly Chronicle,* 26 Aug. 1909, p. 8.
82.   *Cricket and Football Field,* 28 Aug. 1909, p. 8.
83.   Football Association Minutes, 1909.

CHAPTER SEVEN

Spectators

Unlike cricket, which was the "recreation of the classes, of the leisured, and of the men to whom a day or two does not matter," Association football, particularly in its professional, League form was the "game for the millions who can spare an hour or two from the week's work." Of all games, "football gladdens the hearts of the toilers."[1]

The emergence of football as a workingman's game,—the "all-absorbing game of the masses,"[2]—was acknowledged throughout England and in other areas of the world where English patterns of culture spread. Around the turn of the century, Nirad Chaudhuri, who later attended Oxford, recalled that although football was played on occasion in his youth in Bengal, it was regarded as a game "on a rather plebeian level," while there was not "the least room for doubt about the refinement and aristocratic attributes of cricket."[3] The status of football as a working-class pastime was established by the sport's immense popular following and conversely, by the hostility and condescension directed at it from a lofty social plane.

The designation of Association football as a workingman's game encourages an analysis of the political ramifications of the pastime. Gareth Stedman Jones has approached a study of working-class consciousness by examining music halls;[4] in the same way, a study of commercial-professional football provides insights into the ways in which many workers used their leisure time and reveals the techniques employed to preserve extant class relationships. Football serves as an important point of departure for understanding how mass spectator extravaganzas emerged as entertainment, rather than as a potentially disruptive or politically threatening phenomenon. Jones regarded the process by which distinctive working-class pastimes became less threatening to the English ruling class as an expression of the workers' innate apolitical bent.[5] Another explanation for the absence of a politicized working-class culture stresses active upper-class interventions in working-class leisure pursuits.

By the mid-1880s, the industrial working class had supplanted old-boy enthusiasts as football's most devoted and most numerous followers. A reporter who covered the 1886 Association Cup replay in Derby recognized a fundamental shift in the composition of the crowd, and he contrasted the appearance of the spectators with those who had attended the Cup final three years before, when Blackburn Olympic opposed Old Etonians at London's prestigious Kennington Oval:

> On that [earlier] occasion top hats predominated, and it was amusing to hear the "chappies" ejaculate "Pl-ay-ed Eton" or, "Splendidly run, Goodheart." Today the working element are in the majority.[6]

Sir Arthur Hazlerigg commented that in the North and in the Midlands, where factories and workshops proliferated,

> every man is working at very high pressure during every minute of his many hours of employment . . . He has no leisure until his day's work is done [and] every second seems valuable, and the hard worker of indoors becomes a hard player out of doors when his toil is over. If he cannot play himself, he is generally loyal to the club in which he is interested.[7]

Writers who addressed a more genteel audience also noted the changing social composition of football crowds. As the transformation was observed in the early 1880s with the success of Blackburn teams, a writer in the *Pall Mall Gazette* noted, in part facetiously, that London witnessed

> an incursion of Northern barbarians on Saturday—hot-blooded Lancastrians, sharp of tongue, rough and ready, of uncouth garb and speech. A tribe of Sudanese Arabs let loose in the Strand would not excite more amusement and curiousity. . . . Blackburn will turn out in its thousands to welcome back the conquering heroes with bands of music and gay banners. For a few hours, the loom will stand idle, and the sons of toil will drink much more liquor than is good for them.[8]

Descriptions of the enthusiasm exhibited by working-class football supporters abounded. The *Athletic News* depicted the mood in Preston when North End was unexpectedly eliminated from Cup competition in 1887:

> What will those disappointed fellows do, who, since last September, have been paying weekly installments into money clubs to go and see "t' North End i' t' final"? Some of them, who have been in [London] before by working men's trips, had actually planned out their day's enjoyment, and the restaurants they were to show their companions.[9]

In describing the expedition of 2,000 Middlesbrough F.C. supporters to Bradford, a writer for *Cricket and Football Field* stated that it was a

> demonstrative crowd, some of them being in comic attire, others carried rattles, screamers, and other instruments of aural torture, while all, or nearly all, sported the red and white favours of the Ayresome Park club. One youth was attired in a complete suit of the club's colours, while others came in their working garb straight from the blast furnaces or the ship-building yards of Tees-side.[10]

Traveling to other cities to attend football matches had become part of working-class culture, and it was facilitated by the increase in the number of railway lines and trains. In 1913, forty special trains were run from Birmingham to transport 20,000 supporters of the local team to the Cup final in London. The extensive use of railways by football crowds was evident by the 1880s, and the press petitioned railway companies to reduce fares for football charters. The companies were urged to consider "the enormous amount of money" football fans brought "directly to the coffers" of the railways.[11] The rail companies did not reduce fares, but they advertised trips to towns holding important matches. The advertisements began to appear in the early 1890s, and were similar to this promotion of February 1894, which was designed to attract passengers from Lancashire mill towns:

Lancashire and Yorkshire Railway

In Connection With Football Matches Excursion
Tickets Will Be Issued As Follows:—

On Saturday, February 17

From Colne, Nelson, Brierfield, Burnley (Bank Top)
    and Burnley Barracks, to Liverpool
From Waterfoot to Accrington
From Bolton to Darwen
From Blackburn and Mill Hill to Blackpool[12]

Just as weekend football expeditions became a popular habit, so too were the traditions of "good luck" and "welcome home" parades. A journalist who accompanied the Wolverhampton F.C. to London for a Cup final recalled the train's departure, as "thousands of employees from the various works" turned out to wish the team good luck, "waving all sorts of trophies from big sheets to dirty-looking handkerchiefs." For miles,

> chalk marks on the railway wagons, "Play up, Wolves," greeted the eye. And what a reception when the victors got home. A perfect fusilade of fog signals heralded the approach of the train; "Conquering Hero" was being fairly thumped out by the brass band on the other platform, and once the Cup—the best Cup of all—was shown to the thousands outside amid a glare of vari-coloured lights, a ringing, echoing cheer went up, fairly giving one's heart strings tremors.[13]

Similar celebrations occurred each year in the city or town whose team won the Cup competition.[14]

Numerous descriptions of football crowds buttress the hypothesis that commercial-professional football attracted a working-class following. John Hutchinson has attempted to analyze the social composition of the football audience more closely and has tentatively concluded that while workers certainly predominated, those who attended matches were often the more highly skilled and better paid artisans.[15] Hutchinson derived much of his evidence from the police records of the Ibrox Park (Glasgow) disaster of 1902, when the stands collapsed, killing 26 and injuring over 500 spectators. But he acknowledged the inherent limitations with this data, as the match was a special England-versus-Scotland clash, and entrepreneurs had raised the minimum admission price to one shilling. This likely reduced the representation of those patrons who ordinarily attended League matches for 6 d. and who, from other accounts in the press, seem to have constituted the bulk of football's adherents at regular games. The absence of more detailed studies makes it necessary to rely on the impressions of contemporary sportswriters for qualitative data; the consensus among them points to a primarily working-class crowd of both skilled and unskilled workers at football matches. Only occasionally are white-collar and middle-class fans mentioned in these accounts.

An analysis of occupational status among football supporters de-emphasizes the most significant characteristic of football crowds. Whether patrons were operatives or engineers (or, for that matter, clerks or small shopkeepers), they exhibited a willingness to pay for entertainment as it was offered by sports entrepreneurs. As consumers of mass entertainment, all strata of the working class followed a distinct variety of football, the com-mercial-professional game, as it was defined by club directors and reported in the sporting press.

Not all segments of English society approved of the enthusiasm which working-class aficionados displayed for football. For middle- and upper-class writers, class prejudice underlay disdain for football and football crowds. Obvious differences in speech, dress, and general behavior at matches certainly reinforced preexisting cultural biases. In addition to the centuries-old prejudices, specific features of the football mania troubled some middle-class observers. Attendance at midweek matches increased the rate of absenteeism from factory jobs. Wagering and a decline in the physical condition of would-be working-class soldiers prompted some writers to criti-cize the game for facilitating sloth and corruption.

The enthusiasm for football among workers was sufficiently widespread to interrupt factory production. The late nineteenth-century working class was enfranchised and better organized industrially than the one which had experienced a decline in its recreational opportunities a half century earlier, thereby presenting a dilemma to employers. As with operatives in Blackburn whose collective desire to see a match had resulted in the closing of their mill in 1882, iron workers in Sheffield were determined to attend important matches, even at the cost of their wages. Noting the prodigious following of both League clubs in Sheffield, one journalist recalled that workers had asked permission to leave work at the furnaces for an important midweek match. When managers refused permission, the men "went all the same, and now the masters simply accept the inevitable and stop the works."[16]

In Burnley, with the approach of a crucial match against the Tottenham Hotspurs, several industrial establishments closed at noon, "so many of the hands desiring to be at the match.[17] A writer for the *Football Express* estimated that 20,000 looms were stopped in this instance,[18] while a journalist from Bolton reported in 1908 that under similar circumstances "local workshops stopped for the afternoon, and in many cases workpeople took 'French leave.' "[19] In objecting to the scheduling of midweek matches, John Lewis, himself a mill owner, summarized the larger problem of how commercial-professional football interfered with work:

> [A] gentleman told me of a visit he had paid on Monday to a works in Blackburn which he found to be closed down because all the men had gone to see Rovers and Sunderland. In my own case, half my workmen took French leave that afternoon, and I met a manufacturer on Tuesday who was seriously considering the closing of his mill on Saturday morning simply because the men were so busy discussing the coming matches on the afternoons that he could get no work done. It was bad enough, he thought, to have a great deal of time wasted on Mondays in discussing Saturday's matches, and more on Fridays canvassing prospects, organising sweepstakes, and filling up coupons. There is no wonder that employers of labour regard any increase in football fixtures with apprehension, for so many workmen act up to the motto: "if your work interferes with football, give it up."[20]

The *Quarterly Review* included two articles concerning football during the first decade of the twentieth century, and both noted that commercial-professional football hastened a decline in the work ethic. In 1904, a writer complained that "when trade is supposed to be at its worst, thousands of operatives find enough money to attend a match, even if they are on strike."[21] In north Staffordshire factories, the "most dramatic measures" were necessary to keep employees at their work during midweek matches. Another writer for the *Quarterly Review* maintained that attendance at matches was, "in nine cases out of ten," simply an "excuse for loafing or worse."[22] Sir Hiram Maxim, a scientist and inventor, described with dismay the experience of a firm seeking to train native Englishmen as draughtsmen and mathematicians. Although a great number applied,

> as soon as they found out how much there was to learn before they could be called proficient, they became discouraged and grudged the amount of time devoted to their studies. So the greater number "chucked up" the opportunity and again devoted all their spare time to amusements in the form of sports.[23]

The disruption of production was but one contributing factor to the denunciations of commercial-professional football and its working-class crowds in journals with middle- and upper-class readerships. Charles Edwardes, writing in *Nineteenth Century*, mentioned the attendance of a blind person at a football match and offered that the

> gentleman follows the game with his ears. To some of the rest of the spectators [it] would be a positive convenience if they could, on the other hand, during the match, suspend their sense of hearing, as well as their sense of smell. The multitudes flock to the field in their workaday dirt, and with their workaday adjectives loose on their tongues.[24]

A contributor to *Fortnightly Review* asserted that crowds were a "great danger and disadvantage" to football, that the "impetuous mob" grew overwrought at games because the play was "overmuch for their nerves." He complained of "ragged urchins" who would "hoot and yell at anything, however objectionable, that tickles their fancy."[25] The associations that many League club board members had with the liquor trade embarrassed such football officials as William Pickford, who hoped that the game would project a more upstanding image. Pickford disapproved of the drinking bars which proliferated at the entrances to grounds and to the "parade of spirits at half-time behind the grand-stands." He felt that there was "too great a tendency to associate liquor" with football.[26] Ernest Ensor, writing in the *Contemporary Review* in 1898, condemned the "tendency toward brutality" among football spectators. He protested that the "foulest curses of an artisan's vocabulary are shouted" and felt that women were out of place at professional matches. Ensor concluded that the line of demarcation between the upper and lower classes was "growing more distinct" and that "gentlemen can now only play Association football with each other, for they cannot risk plunging into the moral slough."[27]

Ensor's conclusions recall the controversy over professionalism which upset "gentlemen," even after the matter had been resolved by the Football Association in 1885. In an article in the *Saturday Review* in 1888, commercial-professional football was decried as a "show, not a game." The writer denounced what he perceived as the boisterous play among professionals and suggested that amateurs make more frequent appeals to rules committees in order to cleanse the game. He reminded readers that as football was popularized, artisan clubs were founded, "and so football reached the classes from which the professional element in any sport is naturally drawn."[28] Pickford observed that a man could become a professional actor, stockbroker, journalist or novelist and "lose nothing of his social position," but if an individual were a professional athlete, he was "looked down upon."[29]

From the standpoint of some members of the upper classes, then, professional footballers were skillful athletes lacking in character. For most professionals, the "temptation to idle is too strong. The class from which they are drawn is one that neither looks before nor after."[30] By 1886, patrician critics were comparing old-boy football to the newer version, contrasting their styles and ethos:

> Who of those that played in the Cup ties in the "good old days," when all was truly friendly rivalry, would wish to engage in the almost fierce combat which cup ties now engender? Then matches were often played without umpires or referee and in the majority of cases only one arbiter. . . . [In] the majority of ties of the present day, an hostility is generated and an unhealthy excitement prevails which spoils the science of the game and increases the use of brute force.[31]

Wagering was another aspect of football that offended some members of the upper classes. Working-class spectators at football games spent "great sums backing their fancy [with] no regard for the merits of the game and with no real advantage moral or physical to themselves."[32] R. S. S. Baden-Powell, the founder of the Boy Scouts, declared that the huge sums spent in wagering were "an enormous waste of money [among] those who can ill-afford it."[33] Even the sporting press was alarmed at the prevalence of betting on football matches, and reiterated the idea that sports should have moral benefits for the participant, spectator, and society:

> There is one thing about football—or rather one excrescence upon it—that we observe with very keen dread, and that is the increase of betting. . . . One must deplore the ominous increase in the facilities offered to the working classes to indulge in systematic betting.[34]

Disapproval of commercial-professional football was also fueled by broader social, economic, and diplomatic considerations. At a time when England's economic and military stature seemed less certain due to the success of Continental competitors, some members of the governing elite reevaluated various aspects of British society, including recreation.[35] Worker absenteeism prompted by football match attendance not only inspired polemics against what was viewed as sloth, but also provided a further indication to some that a serious flaw in national character was developing at the same pace as were football "gates." Many critics of football embraced the view that England required policies which would foster efficiency on a national scale. Seen in this light, the censure of workers who left factories to attend football games transcended purely moral disapprobation.

A related criticism of football concerned the perceived tendency of workers to watch matches rather than to participate in sports. Writers who expressed doubts about the fighting capacity of the army pointed to the growing attendance at football matches as a poor substitute for more combative recreations that would enhance England's ability to protect or expand her empire. As British imperialism was challenged by German and French expansionism, as the premonition of a European war heightened with the approach of the twentieth century, and as the English ruling class was troubled by the failure to conclude the Boer War easily, the need for an improved fighting force was acknowledged. Passive "spectatorism," it was urged, should be replaced by a more active and utilitarian national policy for recreation.

Advocates of wider participation in games for the purpose of increasing the strength of England's military manpower also drew on the testimony of medical authorities before Parliamentary committees. Reports of social reformers, such as Charles Booth in London's East End and B. Seebohm Rowntree in York, brought to public attention the physical underdevelopment of large sections of the working class, a condition which made them unfit for military service. Consequently, policymakers began to pay more attention to the fitness of the population as a whole. Edward Malins, a Birmingham physician called as a witness before the Inter-Departmental Committee on Physical Deterioration in 1904, equated the growth of football crowds with the decline in standards of physical fitness:

> With regard to outdoor games . . . do you think really the lower classes, especially in larger towns, would themselves go in for outdoor games now?— No.

> As much as their forebears did?—I do not think they would as much.

> They go look at others?—Yes, and do not participate.

> That must be very bad?—You will find a crowd of 15,000 or 20,000 people go to see perhaps thirty players, and then they will go off to drink, as a rule, although it is said they go quietly back home, having enjoyed the fresh air. That is not so. In a town like Birmingham they will give up their work on a Wednesday afternoon to witness a football match. However great the pressure of work in a particular factory may be, I am told nothing would induce them to remain at work if they want to see a football match.[36]

Dr. Malins' coupling of the issue of factory absenteeism with the workers' physical condition lent weight to the increased concern for national efficiency. Essayists worried about the "national physique," as numerous writers urged a regeneration of England's erstwhile enthusiasm for playing. Robert Sturdee, writing in the *Westminster Review* in 1903, observed that the recent tendency had been to

> substitute a passive interest for an active participation in the game. It is not thus that football will redeem our national physique. . . . We want our factory hands to play football for themselves, and not help form a crowd of thousands idly watching others play.

He added that "the Empire will not be maintained by a nation of out-patients."[37] Two years later, T. J. Macnamara urged the government to provide food, housing, and physical training to at least 20 percent of the population. Such largesse, according to Macnamara, should not be based on principles of charity, but rather on the presumption that "Empire cannot be built on rickety and flat-chested citizens."[38]

In a 1909 article entitled "Sport and Decadence," football was condemned as a pastime that corrupted and weakened the work ethic. The article also charged that watching football contributed to England's decline in relation to other countries. It alleged that a nation was on the "downward grade" when a large portion of its population was "incapable of defending" the "motherland" and when the population was

> unable or unwilling to indulge in recreation except vicariously, and regards "sport" as a pastime to be undertaken by others paid for the purpose for the amusement of the onlookers.[39]

The *New Review*, in an article entitled "Are We An Athletic People?" maintained that there "is no civilised country where so small a portion of the population has received a systematic physical training as our own."[40] After citing the rigorous physical training required of young men in Germany and France, the author discussed English enthusiasm for spectator sports:

> It is true that talking about games, and writing about games, and reading about games and looking on at games fill a larger space in the public mind than ever before; but talking, reading, writing, and looking on are not quite the same thing as doing.

A passive approach to sports, as opposed to a more participatory one, 'hardly produces the same result, either on the nation or the individual."[41]

The issue of national physical health and preparedness for war created areas of agreement between those who disparaged professional football (and its supporters) as uncouth, and those who recognized its potential to preserve the status quo. Although several writers for journals with upper-class readerships harbored a subjective dislike for professional football players and the crowds that watched them perform, a desire to shore up the army with healthy conscripts occasionally led them to recognize the benefits of football play. Upper-class observers generally denigrated the atmosphere surrounding commercial-professional football rather than the game itself. They reasoned that if working-class enthusiasts were to play rather than watch football, the nation would reap the benefits. Sir Arthur Conan Doyle, creator of Sherlock Holmes, stated that he had

> known young lads who were disposed to be weak and vacillating rendered thoroughly strong and decided by a course of athletics. I know of no game which is calculated to do more in this respect than football.[42]

Members of the football hierarchy were also quick to point out that English society at large would benefit from the healthful effects of rigorous football play. As early as 1883, James Kerr, a vice-president of the Lancashire Football Association, declared that because of football there were

> a great many thousands of young fellows in Lancashire now capable of enduring an amount of fatigue and exertion that they could not have gone through eight or ten years ago.[43]

C. W. Alcock, a president of the Football Association, had anticipated the call for a national sports policy when in 1891 he and fellow members of the London Playing Field Committee issued their annual report. The report stressed the necessity of redressing the lack of space for football and cricket play in London. The committee further speculated that the "true zeal" displayed by athletes could "hardly be expected to survive many seasons of disappointments, uncertainties, and dangers" that were created by the paucity of facilities; athletes sometimes were unable to obtain any space whatsoever. Policymakers were urged to understand that those who battled for space in crowded Victoria Park might also one day "face the bloodiest battle with absolute indifference."[44]

J. A. H. Catton reported in the *Athletic News* suggestions offered by army officers for increasing the size of the Territorial Forces. Their proposals, submitted to the Football Association in 1913, stressed that the "football community represented the healthy man-power of England, and they, and such as they, were needed for home defense." Catton hoped that the Association would use its influence to found at least a company from each club for the Territorials and declared, "What a service could football render to the Realm!"[45]

In the same column, Catton warned against a false sense of security, wondering whether young men who played football were "ready to fight in defense of the dear homeland, and the fields of their delight, if the helmets of the Germans, or any other nation, confront our eyes?"[46] A writer for the *Birmingham Weekly Post* praised football as a sport which provided physical training. He added that during a time when "wars and rumours of war are prevalent, [football] keeps the race manly, hardy and intelligent."[47] When war did break out in 1914, sportswriters contended that the fighting capacity of soldiers was enhanced through previous participation in football games. Alluding to the health of English recruits, one journalist claimed that the condition of the troops was

> largely due to the culture of the open air life which is so popular with the young manhood of our country. Football and the like have served other ends than mere amusement.[48]

The attitude embraced by some football players differed from that of the sport's officials. Colin Veitch, the chairman of the Players' Union in 1913, responded at length to the suggestion that military training should be made compulsory for football players. For Veitch, the only "shooting" he could condone fell to

> the lot of my feet to perform. When footballers can bring that to perfection, there won't be any danger of lives being lost. . . . I don't mind being hit by a football [but] I cannot bring myself to the same way of thinking where balls of lead are concerned. I object to being hit by such penetrating projectiles, and I have the same objection to hitting anyone else with them.

Veitch stated that he was not alone in this view among players, that there were "many others of similar opinion, and the number is growing."[49]

Veitch's sentiments and Union actions in defiance of football authorities expresed the fundamental division between players and directors. Despite football's reputation as a "workingman's game," officials of the Football Association, the Football League, and individual club directors relied upon popular acceptance of a sport controlled by the bourgeoisie.

Working-class players had gradually recognized the divergence of interests between themselves and the sport's hierarchy, and they eventually organized themselves into a Players' Union to fight for their own betterment. As the rules of the Association and the League came under attack in disputes over player control and in the 1909 strike crisis, football's governors faced the double problem of responding to players' demands while maintaining the enthusiasm for football of the paying crowds.

At a time when the working class came to recognize its own distinct and separate interests and developed such institutions as trade unions and the Labour Party, England's ruling classes faced popular challenges to their attempts to maintain the status quo. If the working class as a whole was beginning to question traditional political and social institutions and practices, to what extent did spectators accept football as it had been developed by entrepreneurs? To what extent, if at all, did spectators, like players, begin to see themselves as mere factors in a larger commercial undertaking?

It is difficult to measure precisely spectator acceptance of commercial-professional football. Attending football matches was one aspect of working-class culture, and working-class spectators witnessed matches in large numbers. They braved the rain and cold weather to stand on crowded, uncovered terraces to see what they could of the action on the field. Covered grandstand seating was available for the price of at least a shilling, but it was generally not affordable for most workers. In spite of the physical discomforts, football matches offered spectators the opportunity to socialize and to appreciate a fine game of football.

The size of football crowds increased dramatically between 1880 and 1914. Football entrepreneurs, perhaps in response to intense competition for the custom of the game's enthusiasts, generally kept ticket prices at a reasonable level. A Football League rule implemented in 1890 standardized terrace admission prices (i.e., minimum prices) at 6 d. for regular League matches, and this statute remained in effect through 1914. Special games, however, could be more expensive to attend. Admission to Football Association Cup final matches was set at a minimum of 1 shilling by the 1880s, and individual teams also raised their prices for cup ties and other special matches. When the Preston North End played at Blackburn in January of 1886, there was "a good deal of grumbling" about the raise in admission fees for this long-awaited match.[50] Even with elevated prices for some matches, spectator enthusiasm ran high and fans came in large numbers to see their favorite clubs play.

The establishment of an admission charge in itself represented an extension of the cash nexus in the area of recreation. Preindustrial football had not required a levy at the "gate" (nor was there a "gate" of any kind!) and had not imposed demands of audience decorum on its spectators. Just as owners now warned players that the traditional roles of "master" and "servant" would be enforced, they reminded spectators that professional matches were not peasant-artisan frolics in which entire villages could participate spontaneously.

Further, to insure that employees of League clubs would observe business rules, clubs installed turnstiles to prevent ticket-takers from pocketing receipts. That this had been a common practice is proven by the fact that at Aston Villa F.C. matches, receipts rose by an average of £175 once turnstiles were installed.[51] New gatekeepers were hired to make certain that those admitted to the Villa ground had actually purchased tickets; in the past the club's loyal followers had merely "tipped the wink" for entree.[52]

Potentially dangerous incidents helped to clarify the obligations of ticket buyers and sellers. Spectators, cramped by an overflow crowd at a 1913 match in Manchester, were pushed onto the field of play. C. E. Sutcliffe scolded both "trespassers" and the Manchester City management, who were otherwise delighted by a turnout which exceeded the seating capacity of their ground. The purchase of a ticket, according to Sutcliffe, implied a "contract between the club and the purchaser" which dictated that the playing field must be "kept clear from the spectators so that all who pay can enjoy the privilege for which they pay."[53] Twenty-five years earlier, the Aston Villa directorate had been accused of jeopardizing the security of players and spectators alike when it failed to provide adequate space around the pitch. Paying customers crowded around the playing area, prompting one journalist to remark that the Villa directors "knew they would have a tremendous crowd, but with the idea of scooping in all the money they could, they did not go to much expense" in securing the playing field.[54]

According to those who controlled the sport, providing mass entertainment spectacles could have a stabilizing effect on the working class. Without responding directly to critics of "spectatorism" or to writers who disapproved of the "crude" habits of club supporters, football's defenders contended that match attendance kept potentially disruptive classes off the streets, providing "innocent recreation for a couple of hours each week for men who might otherwise be in worse places."[55] A writer stated that a "working man" informed him that he certainly would attend a partcular match. The worker was quoted as having said,

> Of course, I shall be there. Do you know what I tell my mates? Why, that football is the grandest thing that ever came out for the likes of me, because it enables us to forget all the cares, troubles and ills of life for two or three hours every Saturday. I'd sooner miss the old woman's best Sunday dinner than a match on Saturday. And the old girl likes me to go for she knows I'm not doing any harm there.[56]

Although it does not seem likely that a workingman would volunteer such rhapsodic prose on the benefits of attending football matches to a newspaper reporter, the presence of such views in the sporting press illustrates how the game could be recommended as a vehicle for social control.

Despite the extensive sale of alcoholic beverages at matches, football was recommended as a boon to the temperance movement by the game's defenders. A Football Association official in Liverpool reasoned that dock workers tended to "rush home from work and hand over their wages before going to the match" during the winter months. During the summer, however, there was a tendency among these men to "spend their money before they reached home," often at a pub.[57] In response to one clergyman's allegation that working-class support of football was a "waste," a writer referred to (unidentified) "chief constables of the land" who could prove by official statistics that convictions for drunkenness on Saturdays diminished where professional football matches were played.

This writer transcended what may be termed the "temperance defense" of commercial-professional football by mentioning another, more fundamental point concerning the game's value. He added that

> we fail to see that money spent on recreation which refreshes the jaded workman, which relieves the monotony of life, which lends colour to the drab days of weary weeks, is waste. The workman is all the better for such a mean pursuit.[58]

This theme resounded in the sporting press with some frequency. In Derby, a writer claimed that football diverted people from "all those wearing and harrassing matters which are incidental to everyday existence."[59] Football League president William McGregor cautioned players during the 1909 strike crisis not to puncture the illusions of the public and reveal football as a business through their open resistance to team owners. Football, stated McGregor, "is a sport in the eyes of those who pay to watch it." Results would be contrary to expectations if the Players' Union succeeded in having football "recognised as a business pure and simple, because they will then have precious few of the British public to watch them play."[60]

Even the more genteel press understood football's function in working-class communities. While football crowds exhibited behavior that might offend middle-class tastes, it was impossible to ignore the fact that attending matches provided harmless excitement for people who might well have turned their energies to far more threatening activities. Ernest Ensor, writing in the *Contemporary Review* in 1898, observed that when

> the misery of a long, cruel strike has settled down upon a manufacturing district, and the actual pinch of famine is being felt by nearly everyone, the sums taken at the big football matches do not fall off in the same proportion as all other receipts from the starving people. Threepence or sixpence are hoarded up all week in order that the mind may have its brief period of excitement and uplifiting, which makes up for the weary, sordid days of the past week. The astonishing increase in the numbers that play and watch others play the great English games is largely due to the dull monotony of life in our large towns; it is the absolute necessity of some change, some interest outside the daily work, which has ceased to be interesting, that causes the huge crowds at the weekly football matches.[61]

Decades before, some upper-class opponents of industrialization had expressed the belief that sports and other traditional pastimes helped to maintain a social equilibrium, and the decline of preindustrial plebeian football had troubled some who in all probability did not play the game themselves.[62] Joseph Ellison of Bradford, testifying before the Select Committee on the Health of Towns in 1840, commented that he was

> happy to say that Chartism* is very rapidly dying away, but if the lower orders have not places where they can engage in sports, it is the very thing to drive them to Chartism; there cannot be a better thing than to keep their minds engaged in matters of that kind.[63]

Robert Slaney, an M.P. who expressed misgivings about the decline of traditional recreations with the spread of industrialization, commented that it was "alike wise and benevolent to provide, in regulated amusements for the many, safety valves for their energies." The absence of such "safety valves," predicted Slaney, would cause the working class to "fly to demagogues and dangerous causes."[64] At the turn of the twentieth century, close to sixty years after Ellison and Slaney had stated their apprehensions, Robert Sturdee supported the view that games such as football effectively diverted the working population and that one could

> wish that they were all engaged in the game themselves, but even these advantages are not to be despised. Better to be an idle spectator under these conditions than remain idle in the slums.[65]

The case for perceiving football as an "opiate" emerges from these statements by contemporaries. Commercial-professional football, like other entertainments controlled and financed by the bourgeoisie, arguably created a safety valve through which pressure generated by industrial capitalism could pass safely, without endangering the basic relationships of society.

While a variety of other factors militated against radical working-class initiatives around the turn of the twentieth century, the conscious efforts of entrepreneurs to structure and influence recreational opportunities should not be overlooked. The appearance of commercialized leisure activities helps to account at least in a small way for the passivity of many workers. The view that external factors impinged on the impulse to alter social and political conditions contradicts Gareth Stedman Jones's hypothesis that there were inherent limitations on working-class militancy which were expressed in the proletariat's choice of leisure activities. Although Jones' study of music halls revealed an apolitical bent among workers, other evidence shows that considerable pressure was applied to promote nondisruptive programs which tended to normalize extant class relationships. In Birmingham, for instance, a writer urged that music halls

> might be made, and ought to be made, a great educational agent for the lower middle and working classes who are its chief patrons. . . . Everything should be done that can be done to foster and facilitate rational entertainment that is harmless, and inoffensive to public decency.[66]

---

*Chartism was a nineteenth-century English movement which advocated better social, political, and economic conditions for the working class.

In Liverpool, a writer maintained that while a gentleman should not take his wife or sister to a music hall and that the entertainment there was altogether low-brow,

> recreation is necessity to the toiler, and the music hall tries to supply it to the class it caters for. The entertainment provided will doubtless admit of much improvement, but indecent song, and suggestive actions, is the exception and not the rule on music hall boards, and managers are properly aware that such a deportment would soon endanger their licence.[67]

Peter Bailey concurred that the content of music hall entertainment and their general ambience were dictated less by working-class patrons than by music hall operators whose partial goal was the "improvement" of the masses.[68] As such, the spread of music hall entertainment might best be a measure of the middle-class response to the increase in worker leisure time, rather than a barometer of innate working-class attitudes toward politics.

As norms of behavior were in part dictated by music hall proprietors, so too, was behavior prescribed by a hierarchy for football matches. Vamplew has described how Association and League officials disseminated rules for football crowd behavior, with injunctions against disorderly demonstrations, crowding too close to the pitch, and betting. Although these statutes were frequently ignored by patrons, their appearance seems consistent with the desires of other leisure entrepreneurs.[69] More fundamentally, businessmen directors simultaneously instituted such practices as wage payments to players and the charging of admission fees into the operation of football teams.

It may indeed be appropriate to reconsider the value of designating football a "workingman's game" in anything other than a superficial sense. To be sure, workingmen constituted the labor force in commercial-professional football and attended matches in great numbers. However, the working class did not control when or where professional football was played, nor, as paid players or paying spectators, did working people determine the sharing of revenue generated by football enterprises. The predication of the game on a system of wage labor and the necessary purchase of admission rights to matches reproduced entrepreneurial control of economic life in the cultural realm. The bitter battles for control of commercial-professional football waged by team directors since the 1880s attest to the determination of the middle class to structure football along business lines.

In a somewhat narrower sense, football matches provided convenient forums for encouraging working-class acceptance of the traditional electoral system and parties. In an age when the political elite in England found it essential that "means of cultivating support of urban working men" be found,[70] football served as a useful instrument for creating illusions among working people regarding the intentions and inclinations of candidates. Many a politician found it beneficial to spend a Saturday afternoon campaigning at the football ground. By exploiting the opiate football, he could pretend a genuine concern for and interest in players and spectators. Robert Tressell, in *The Ragged Trousered Philanthropists* (1911), described a working class that was content to watch football games rather than to confront the causes of its poverty, and which showed a willingness to swallow the notion that candidates who appeared at football matches therefore truly represented their interests.[71] While Tressell was dismayed, others either applauded or were amazed by the football mania. In 1909, a magistrate in Birmingham remarked that "people were 'stark staring football mad.' They paid more attention to football than to the Finance Bill."[72]

Although it probably did not typify the behavior of most politicians or club directors, the Middlesbrough F.C. scandal of 1910 illustrated the uses to which football could be put. The Middlesbrough chairman, Colonel T. Gibson Poole, recruited his players to canvass and speak for him in his ultimately unsuccessful Conservative candidacy for Parliament. Bribe money to Sunderland F.C. players, whose defeat at the hands of Middlesbrough was though to have enhanced Poole's electoral chances, was traced to Poole by the Football Association.[73] Some football directors were more successful at election time. Samuel Hill Wood, the principal shareholder of the Glossop F.C., was a member of Parliament, as was Arthur Kynoch, president of the Aston Villa F.C. board until 1888.

As early as 1882, politicians were present at football matches. Generally, their attendance was noted by the press at more celebrated matches which attracted the largest crowds and the widest newspaper coverage. An editor for *Pastime,* a London publication, observed that in northern counties,

> candidates of both parties during the recent electoral struggles were assiduous in courting the favour of players by attending the principal matches, and making a great show of their interest in the game.[74]

M.P.s appeared at season-opening matches and at special midweek games. Arthur Balfour and Lord Rosebery were among the prominent politicians who attended Cup finals during the 1890s, beginning a tradition that has continued to this day. At a West Bromwich Albion-Aston Villa Cup final played in London in 1887, politics and football were combined. West Bromwich M.P. J. Ernest Spencer invited the players from the Albion side to dinner in order to wish them luck. Not to be outdone, the M.P. for the Aston Villa district issued a similar invitation to the Villa squad. The prematch political "competition" was not lost on the press. "Who would have thought a few years ago," asked a writer for *Sports and Play,*

> that real live M.P.s would be inviting football teams to be dining with them in London? Since the days of our youth the game has gone up in public estimation with a vengeance.[75]

To be sure, there was nothing particularly sinister or surprising about politicians campaigning amidst large crowds; football matches simply were obvious places for electioneering. With the passage of reform legislation and the expansion of the electorate, politicians were increasingly preoccupied with attracting new voters to the traditional political parties. This entailed the creation of such new campaign techniques as establishing direct contact with workingmen to insure that preexisting policies would receive their support. At a match in Sunderland, for instance, it was observed that the "British working man grimed by recent toil—there was no time for a wash and a 'snack'—stood cheek by jowl with his worship the Mayor and Colonel Gourley, M.P."[76] Ernest Ensor noted that a Cup final was a larger spectacle than an ordinary football match. As if to emphasize the class divisions in English society, he stated that such an important match "draws together people who would otherwise never rub shoulders."[77]

Football as a sport and business enterprise transcended the realm of goal scoring on a pitch. Its usefulness to politicians was but one example of football's potential for maintaining a consensus.

Notes

1. *Athletic News,* 2 Sept. 1901, p. 1.

2. *Football Mail* (Newcastle), 23 Jan. 1904, p. 1.

3. Nirad C. Chaudhuri, *The Autobiography of an Unknown Indian* (New York: Macmillan, 1951), p. 109.

4. Gareth Stedman Jones, "Working-Class Culture," passim.

5. Ibid., p. 462 and passim.

6. *Athletic News,* 13 April 1886, p. 4.

7. *Football Echo* (Sunderland) 20 March 1909, p. 3.

8. *Pall Mall Gazette* (London), 31 March 1884, p. 11.

9. *Athletic News,* 8 March 1887, p. 1.

10. *Cricket and Football Field,* 10 Jan. 1914, p. 9.

11. *Sports and Play,* 1 Oct. 1889, p. 558.

12. *Athletic News,* 12 Feb. 1894, p. 4.

13. *Athletic News,* 27 March 1893, p. 5.

14. See the *Blackburn Times* of 7 April 1883, for instance, for a report of the hysteria throughout the town after Blackburn Olympic won the Cup.

15. Hutchinson's findings are contained in his paper, "Some Aspects of Football Crowds Before 1914." I am indebted to Professor Wray Vamplew from the Flinders University of South Australia for making Mr. Hutchinson's paper available to me.

16. *Athletic News,* 6 Feb. 1893, p. 1.

17. *The Burnley Gazette and East Lancashire Advertiser* (Burnley), 27 Feb. 1909, p. 3.

18. *The Football Express,* 27 Feb. 1909, p. 10.

19. *Bolton Evening News,* 5 Feb. 1908, p. 4.

20. *Football Mail* (Hartlepool), 28 March 1914, p. 1.

21. *Quarterly Review* (London), Jan. 1904, p. 138.

22. *Quarterly Review,* Oct. 1909, p. 495.

23. *Football Express,* 6 Feb. 1909, p. 3.

24. *Nineteenth Century* (London), Oct. 1892, p. 627.

25. *Fortnightly Review* (London), 1 Jan. 1894, p. 33.

26. *Football Echo* (Sunderland), 9 Jan. 1909, p. 1.

27. *Contemporary Review,* Nov. 1898, pp. 758, 760.

28. *Saturday Review* (London), 14 April 1888, p. 437.

29. *Football Echo* (Sunderland), 9 Jan. 1909, p. 1.

30. *Contemporary Review,* Nov. 1898, p. 754.

31. *Pastime,* 27 Jan. 1886, p. 49.

32. *Quarterly Review,* Oct. 1909, p. 501.

33. *Bolton Evening News,* 8 Feb. 1908, p. 4.

34. *Cricket and Football Field,* 20 March 1909, p. 1.

35. G. R. Searle, in *The Quest for National Efficiency* (Berkeley: University of California Press, 1971) describes how various sectors within English society recognized and responded to the loss of international commercial, industrial, and military hegemony.

36. Interdepartmental Committee on Physical Deterioration, *Parliamentary Papers,* 1904, vol. XXXII, p. 139.

37. *Westminister Review* (London), Feb. 1903, p. 181.

38. *Contemporary Review,* Feb. 1905, p. 248.

39. *Quarterly Review,* Oct. 1909, p. 489.

40. *New Review* (London), Jan. 1897, p. 42.

41. Ibid., p. 43, 45.

42. *Manchester Evening Chronicle,* 3 Oct., 1908, p. 6.

43. *Preston Herald,* 30 May 1883, p. 6.

44. *London Playing Fields Committee First Annual Report,* 1891, p. 14.

45. *Athletic News,* 17 March 1913, p. 4.

46. Ibid.

47. *Birmingham Weekly Post,* 1 Sept. 1900, p. 22.

48. *Football Post* (Nottingham), 3 Oct. 1914, p. 8.

49. *Football Players Magazine,* Feb. 1913, p. 13.

50. *Athletic News,* 5 Jan., 1886, p. 1.

51. Peter Morris, *Aston Villa* (London: Naldrett Press, 1960), p. 29.

52. *The Athlete,* 28 Dec. 1885, p. 826.

53. *Athletic News,* 10 Feb. 1913, p. 4.

54. *Athletic Journal,* 10 Jan. 1888, p. 9.

55. *Football and Sports Special,* 20 March 1909, p. 4.

56. *Athletic News,* 5 Sept. 1910, p. 1.

57. *Liverpool Football Echo,* 20 Feb. 1909, p. 2.

58. *Athletic News,* 20 Feb. 1911, p. 1.

59. *Football Express,* 23 Jan. 1909, p. 3.

60. *Football Echo* (Sunderland), 3 April 1909, p. 1.

61. *Contemporary Review,* Nov. 1898, pp. 752–753.

62. Malcolmson amplified this point in *Popular Recreations,* chaps. 5 and 6.

63. Select Committee on the Health of Towns, *Parliamentary Papers,* 1840, vol. XI, p. 92.

64. Cited in Bailey, *Leisure and Class in Victorian England,* p. 36.

65. *Westminister Review,* Feb. 1903, p. 182.

66. *Birmingham Daily Mail,* 24 Aug. 1888, p. 2.

67. *Liverpool Review,* 15 Oct. 1892, p. 14.

68. Bailey, *Leisure and Class in Victorian England,* Ch. 7.

69. Wray Vamplew, "Ungentlemanly Conduct: The Control of Soccer-Crowd Behaviour in England, 1888–1914," in T. C. Smout, ed., *The Search for Wealth and Stability* (London: Macmillan, 1979), pp. 143, 149.

70. Paul Smith, *Disraelian Conservatism and Social Reform* (London: Routledge & Kegan Paul, 1967), p. 29.

71. Robert Tressell, *The Ragged Trousered Philanthropists* (London: Granada, 1979), pp. 18, 527, 542.

72. *Sports Argus,* 7 Aug. 1909, p. 8.

73. Football Association Minutes, 1910.

74. *Pastime,* 17 Feb. 1886, p. 94.

75. *Sports and Play,* 21 March 1887, p. 227.

76. *Athletic News,* 23 Dec. 1889, p. 4.

77. *Contemporary Review,* Nov. 1898, p. 752.

Conclusion

The hoopla and hysteria surrounding football served to obscure the game's structure and purposes. Newspapers stressed the heroics of individual players and teams and generally failed to analyze football either historically or sociologically. Predictably, sportswriters treated football as mere entertainment and consequently confined themselves to enlightening the public about brilliant dashes and flashy saves.

Present-day scholars have observed the significance of football in English society and have viewed the game from a different perspective. Recently, academics have analyzed football as an aspect of working-class culture, a diversion for one section of the population. The language, dress, and general demeanor of football supporters have consitututed worthwhile areas of inquiry in attempts to ascertain broader attitudes of the proletariat.

What might be stressed further in a composite sketch of football supporters and players is an analysis of the fundamental relationships on which commercial-professional football was based. The presence of paid performers and the dichotomy between players and spectators too often have been taken for granted. The extension of a cash nexus between club directors and spectators, and directors and players, is a central theme of the present discusssion of football which constitutes a partial corrective to the emphasis on other more apparent dimensions which have provided the focus for other studies.

A study of the football business corroborates the value of utilizing a class analysis to explicate aspects of popular culture. Commercial-professional football replicated prevailing class arrangements insofar as club directors drawn from the bourgeoisie employed working-class players for a wage. With the extension of more leisure time to the English working class in the 1860s and 1870s, entrepreneurs grasped the emerging possibilities of leisure and recreational enterprises. Football represented one such opportunity for businessmen, and the game was sold as entertainment by the early 1880s.

The market forces which generated and guided such recreations as commercialized football in turn dictated the need for professional players. The relations between owners and professionals determined the degree of calm or tension in big-time football. While sportswriters often were able simply to report matches and revel in football minutiae, they increasingly were obliged to describe player-owner disputes reminiscent of the quarrels between labor and capital off the football pitch.

From this picture of the commercial-professional game, it becomes clear that some heretofore popular labels for football are misleading. For instance, football's status as a "game for the masses" might be revised with the recognition that "the masses" did not control the operation of matches at the highest levels of the sport. So, too, must the notion of football serving as a "democratizing" influence be reconsidered. It was true that most class distinctions were levelled on the actual field of play and that football after the third quarter of the nineteenth century drew participants from various classes. Indeed, this pattern contrasted sharply with prior recreational tendencies, wherein different classes engaged in separate pastimes. However, on closer examination, it becomes evident that for big-time football, at least, class roles and relationships were made to conform with those of ordinary life.

Bibliography

Primary Sources

Newspapers and Periodicals

The Athlete (Birmingham)
Athletic and Dramatic News (Liverpool)
Athletic Journal (Manchester)
Athletic News (Manchester)
Athletic News Football Annual (Manchester)
Badminton Magazine of Sports and Pastimes (London)
Bat and Ball (Manchester)
Bell's Life in London (London)
Birmingham Daily Mail
Birmingham Weekley Post
Blackburn Times
Bolton Chronicle
Bolton Evening Chronicle
Bolton Evening News
Bolton Journal and Guardian
Burnley Gazette and East Lancashire Advertiser
Chambers Journal (London)
Contemporary Review (London)
Cricket and Football Field (Bolton)
Derby and Chesterfield Reporter (Derby)
Derby and Derbyshire Gazette (Derby)
Eastern Daily Press (Norwich)
English Illustrated Magazine (London)
The Field (London)
Football (London)
Football (Wolverhampton)
Football and Sports Special (Sheffield)
Football Annual (Manchester)
Football Chronicle and Athletic Advertiser (Grantham)
Football Echo (Sunderland)
Football Express (Derby)
Football Field and Sports Telegram (Bolton)
Football Mail (Hartlepool)

Football Mail (Newcastle)
Football News (Nottingham)
Football Pink 'Un (Birmingham)
Football Players Magazine (Manchester)
Football Post (Nottingham)
Fortnightly Review (London)
Gamage's Association Football Annual (London)
Land and Water (London)
Lacedemonian Mercury (London)
Lincoln Gazette and Lincolnshire Times
Lincolnshire Chronicle and General Advertiser (Lincoln)
Liverpool Football Echo
Liverpool Review
Manchester Evening Chronicle
Manchester Evening News Football Handbook
Midland Athletic Star (Birmingham)
New Review (London)
Newcastle Daily Journal
Newcastle Weekly Chronicle
Nineteenth Century (London)
Northern Athlete (Newcastle)
Pall Mall Gazette (London)
Pastime (London)
Penny Magazine (London)
Preston Chronicle
Preston Guardian
Preston Herald
Quarterly Review (London)
Railway Review (London)
Saturday Review (London)
The Scotsman (Edinburgh)
Sheffield Daily Telegraph
Sheffield Guardian
The Spectator (London)
Sporting Chronicle (Manchester)
Sporting Life (London)
Sports and Play (Birmingham)
Sports Argus (Birmingham)
The Times (London)
Truth (London)
Westminster Review (London)
World's Work (London)

Minutes and Reports

First Annual Report, London Playing Fields Committee, 1891
Football Association Minutes
Football League Minutes
Professional Footballers Association Minutes
"Report from the Inter-Departmental Commission on Physical Deterioration." *Parliamentary Papers*, 1904, vol. XXXII.
"Report from the Select Committee on the Health of Towns." *Parliamentary Papers*, 1840, vol. XI.
"Report from the Select Committee on Public Walks." *Parliamentary Papers*, 1833, vol. XV.
"Report from Commissioners, Children's Employment Commission." *Parliamentary Papers,* 1843, vols. XIV, XV.

Books

Alcock, C. W. *Association Football.* London: George Bell and Sons, 1890.
The Book of Football. London: Amalgamated Press, 1906.
Catton, J. A. H., *The Real Football.* London: Sands & Co., 1900.
Football Calendar. London: Wright & Co., 1893.
Football's Who's Who. London: C. Arthur Pearson, 1902.
Hughes, Thomas, *Tom Brown's School Days.* New York: Macmillan, 1910.
Jackson, N. L., *Association Football.* London: George Newnes, 1899.
Men Famous in Football. London: Bedford Pub., 1903.
Pickford, William, *A Few Recollections of Sport.* London: Football Association, 1913.
Pickford, William and Alfred Gibson, *Association Football and the Men Who Made It.* London: Caxton, 1905.
Shearman, Montague, *Badminton Library of Sports and Pastimes: Athletics and Football.* London: Spottiswoode & Co., 1889.
Strutt, Joseph, *The Sports and Pastimes of the People of England.* London: 1801; reprint ed., Bath: Firecrest Pub., 1969.
Sutcliffe, C. E., *The Story of the Football League.* Preston: Football League, Ltd., 1938.

Secondary Sources

"An Eighteenth Century Inclosure and Football Play at West Haddon," *Northamptonshire Past and Present* (1968/1969).
Appleton, Arthur, *Hotbed of Soccer: The Story of Football in the Northeast.* London: Hart-Davis, 1961.

Brailsford, Dennis, *Sport and Society: Elizabeth to Anne.* London: Routledge & Kegan Paul, 1969.

Bailey, Peter, *Leisure and Class in Victorian England: Rational Recreation and the Contest for Control, 1830–1885.* London: Routledge & Kegan Paul, 1978.

Burke, Peter, *Popular Culture in Early Modern Europe.* London: Maurice Temple Smith, 1978.

Caillois, Roger, *Man, Play and Games.* New York: Free Press, 1961.

Churchill, R. C., *Sixty Seasons of League Football.* London: Penguin, 1958.

Douglas, Peter, *The Football Industry.* London: George Allen & Unwin, 1973.

Dunning, Eric, "Industrialization and the Incipient Modernization of Football," *Arena* (1975).

Glanville, Brian, *Soccer.* New York: Crown, 1958.

Govett, L. A., *The King's Book of Sports.* London: Elliot Stock, 1890.

Green, Geoffrey, *The History of the Football Association.* London: Naldrett Press, 1953.

Hammond, J. L., *The Growth of Common Enjoyment.* London: Oxford University Press, 1933.

Hill, Jimmy, *Striking for Soccer.* London: P. Davis, 1961.

Huizinga, Johan, *Homo Ludens: A Study of the Play Element in Culture.* Boston: Beacon Press, 1950.

Jones, Gareth Stedman, "Class Expression *Versus* Social Control?" *History Workshop* (Autumn 1977).

Jones, Gareth Stedman, "Working-Class Culture and Working-Class Politics in London, 1870–1900: Notes on the Remaking of a Working Class," *Journal of Social History* (Summer 1974).

Joy, Bernard, *Forward, Arsenal!* London: Phoenix, 1952.

Keates, Thomas, *The History of the Everton F.C.* Liverpool: Thomas Brakell, Ltd., 1928.

Keeton, George, *The Football Revolution: A Study of the Changing Pattern of Association Football.* Devon: David and Charles, 1972.

Loy, John, and Gerald Kenyon, *Sport, Culture and Society: A Reader on the Sociology of Sport.* New York: Macmillan, 1969.

MacGregor, Robert, *Pastimes and Players.* London: Chatto and Windus, 1881.

McIntosh, P. C., *Sport in Society.* London: C. A. Watts, 1963.

Magoun, Francis P., "Football in Medieval England and Middle English Literature," *American Historical Review* (October 1929).

Magoun, Francis P., "The History of Football from the Beginnings to 1871," *Kolner-Anglistische Arbeiten.* Bochum-Langendreer, 1938.

Malcolmson, Robert W., *Popular Recreations in English Society 1700–1850.* Cambridge: University Press, 1973.

Marples, Morris, *A History of Football.* London: Secker and Warburg, 1954.

Molyneux, Denis, "The Development of Physical Recreation in the Birmingham District from 1871–1892," unpublished M.A. thesis. Birmingham: University of Birmingham, 1957.

Morris, Peter, *Aston Villa.* London: Naldrett Press, 1960.

Morris, Peter, *West Bromwich Albion: Soccer in the Black Country.* London: Heinemann, 1965.

Plumb, J. H., *The Commercialisation of Leisure in Eighteenth Century England.* Reading: University of Reading, 1973.

Thomspon, Edward P., "Patrician Society, Plebeian Culture," *Journal of Social History* (Summer 1974).

Thompson, Edward P., "Time, Work-Discipline and Industrial Capitalism," *Past and Present* (December 1967).

Vamplew, Wray, "Playing for Pay: The Earnings of Professional Sportsmen in England 1870–1914," paper to the Conference on the Making of Sporting Traditions, University of New South Wales, 1979.

Vamplew, Wray, "The Sport of Kings and Commoners: The Commercialization of Horse-Racing in the Nineteenth Century," in R. I. Cashman, and M. McKernan, *Sport and History.* Queensland: Queensland University Press, 1979.

Vamplew, Wray, "Ungentlemanly Conduct: The Control of Soccer-crowd Behaviour in England, 1888–1914," in T. C. Smout, (ed.), *The Search for Wealth and Stability.* London: Macmillan, 1979.

Walvin, James, *Leisure and Society 1830–1950.* London: Longman's, 1978.

Walvin, James, *The People's Game.* London: Allen Lane, 1974.

Weiss, Paul, *Sport: A Philosophic Inquiry.* Carbondale: Southern Illinois University Press, 1969.

Young, Percy M., *Football on Merseyside.* London: Stanley Paul, 1963.

Young, Percy M., *Manchester United.* London: Heinemann, 1960.

Young, Percy M., and Derek Dougan, *On the Spot: Football as a Profession.* London: Stanley Paul, 1974.

Index